THE WISDOM OF MOM:
WORDS OF LOVE AND ENCOURAGEMENT

CELTIC COLORING BOOK

AUDREY O'SHEA

Use this page and the previous one to practice your colors.
(There are also some practice pages in the back.)

With 37 Celtic inspired large images plus many smaller ones this book will give you hours of relaxation as you express your creativity through color, and contemplate the encouraging and positive thoughts on the opposite pages.

Large pictures are on only one side of the page so that you could color them with markers and not worry about bleeding through and ruining another large image. If you're using markers, you might want to put a blank paper behind the page you're coloring just to make sure.

ISBN: 1533664285
ISBN-13: 978-1533664280

Welcome: I was lucky to have an amazing mom. She did all the "normal" mom things like bandage boo-boos and take us to piano lessons, but unlike some of the other moms that I knew, my mom always approached things from a place of love toward everyone, even when we were in trouble. She taught me and my siblings to love and respect each other and ourselves, *and* to make our beds.

This book is my way of sharing that love with you. I hope that as you read the words on the pages that follow and color the pictures you will find peace, happiness, and some ideas to keep and make your own; something to nourish your soul.

:) Be Happy
Audrey

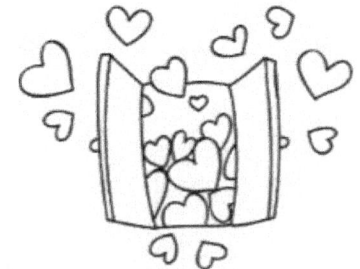

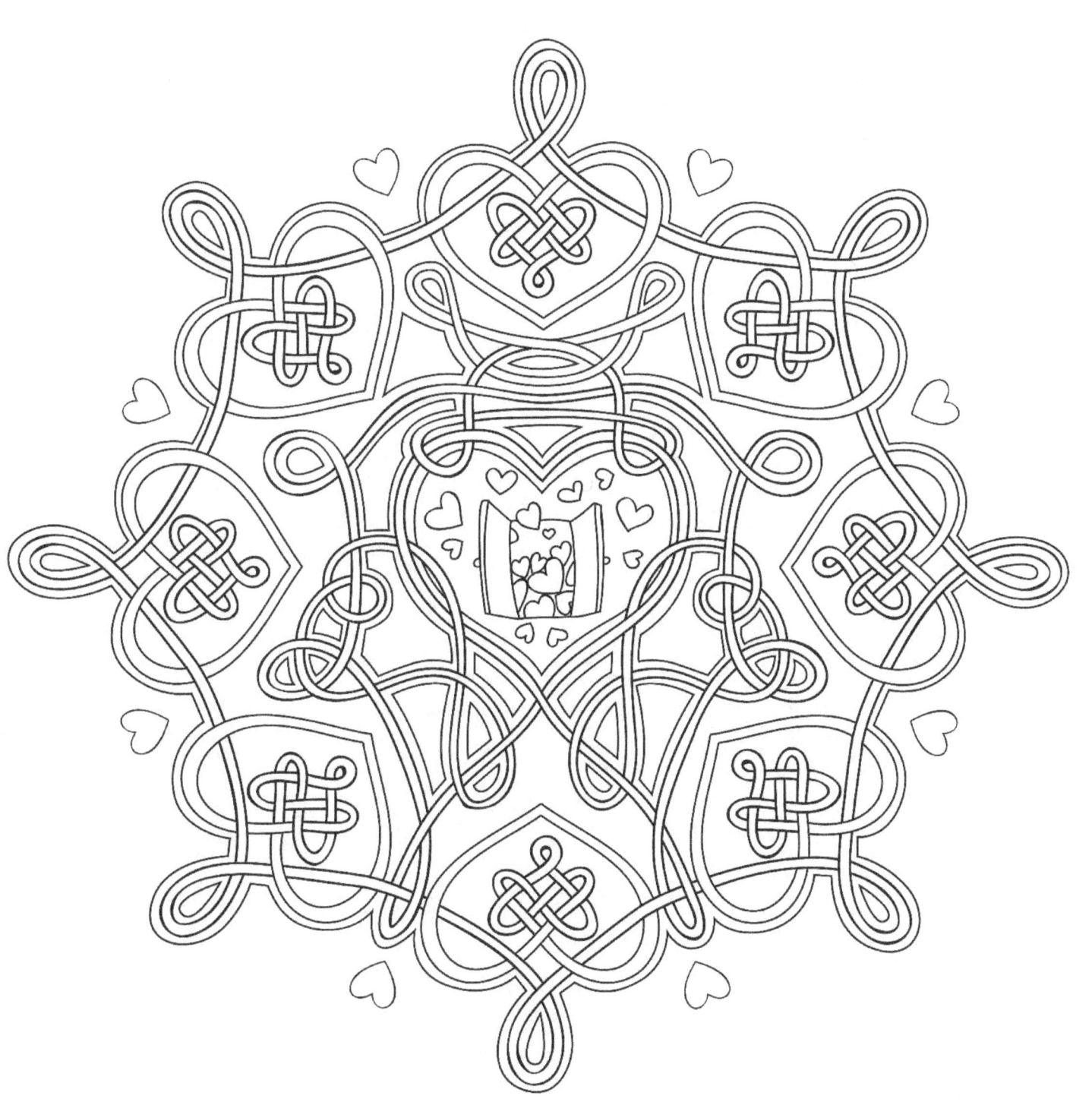

You Matter: When you put a puzzle together you have just enough pieces to get it done. You are a piece of the puzzle that makes this thing we call life. Without you the puzzle would be incomplete. You are, therefore, a very important person.

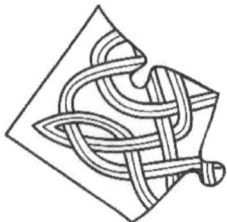

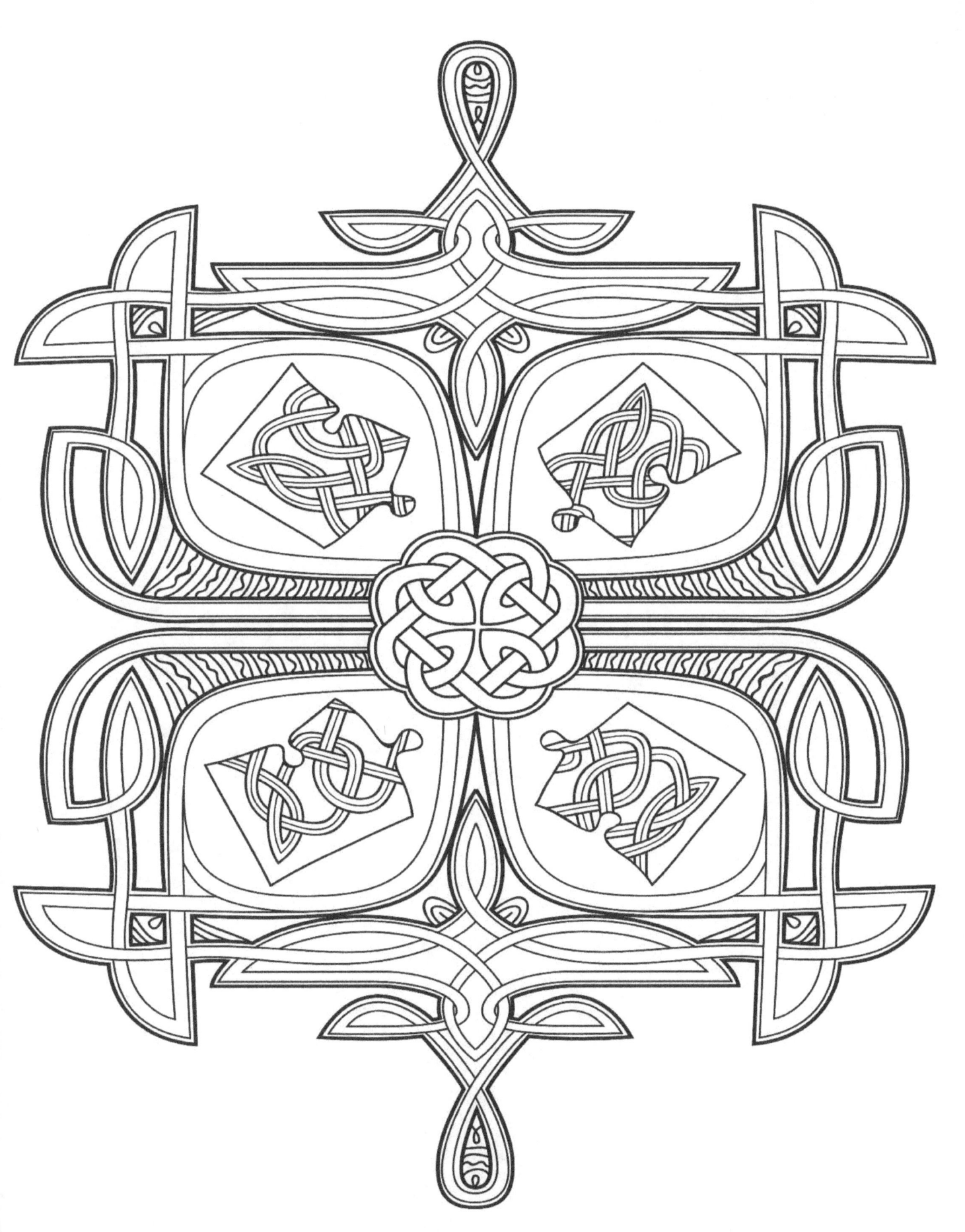

Life Can Be Hard: Sometimes people break hearts. It happens to everyone. It may be intentional or not, but sooner or later it will happen to you. You feel like you're not going to make it through but hang in there, it will get better.

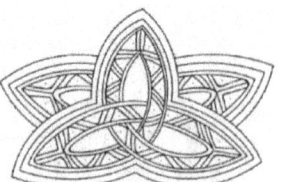

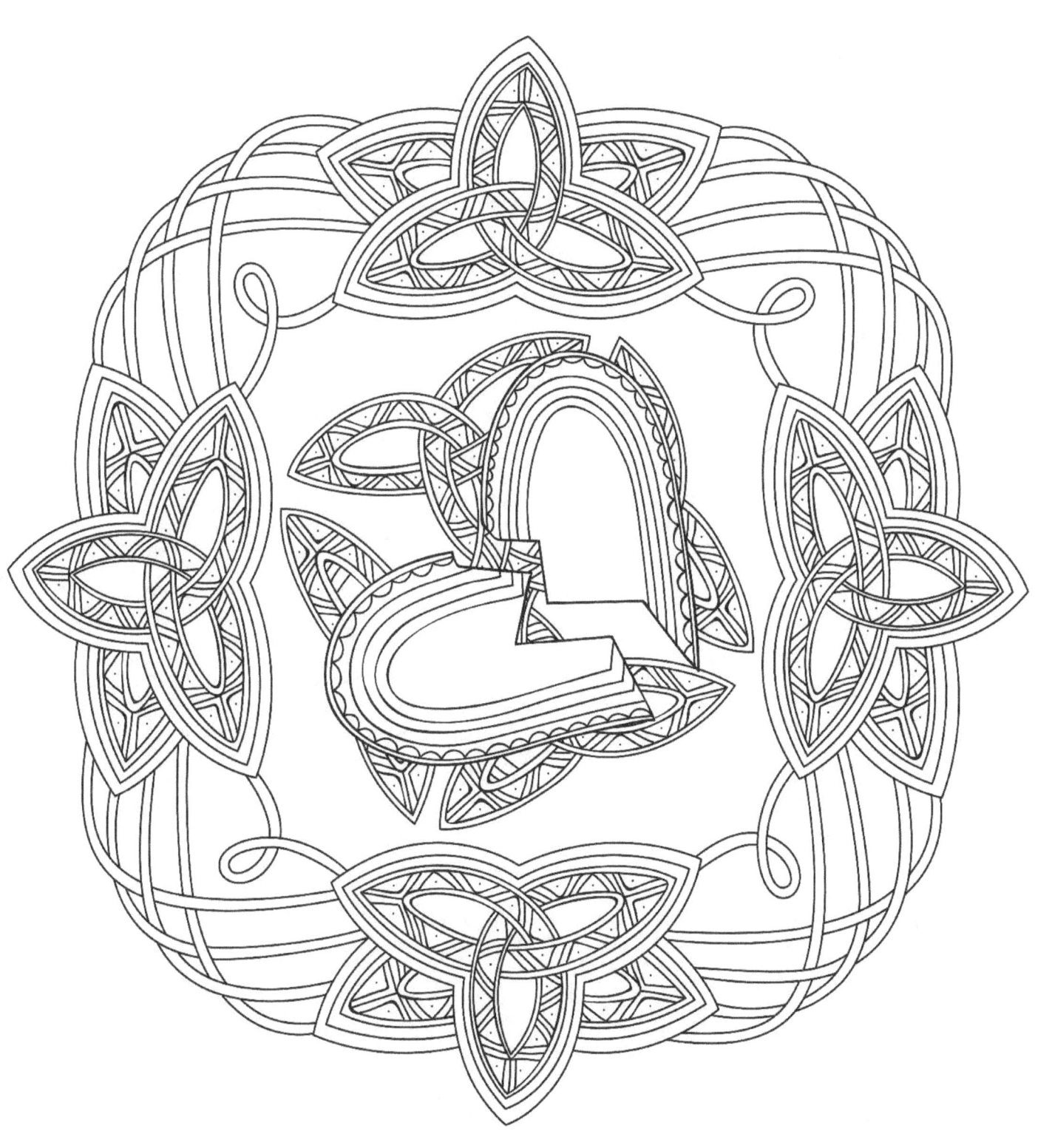

It Will Get Better: No matter how good or bad it is, life will change. The sun keeps coming up even when you feel like you're going to just die of a broken heart. Eventually the pain will ease, your heart will mend, and you will find a way to smile again.

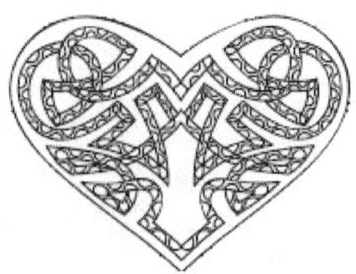

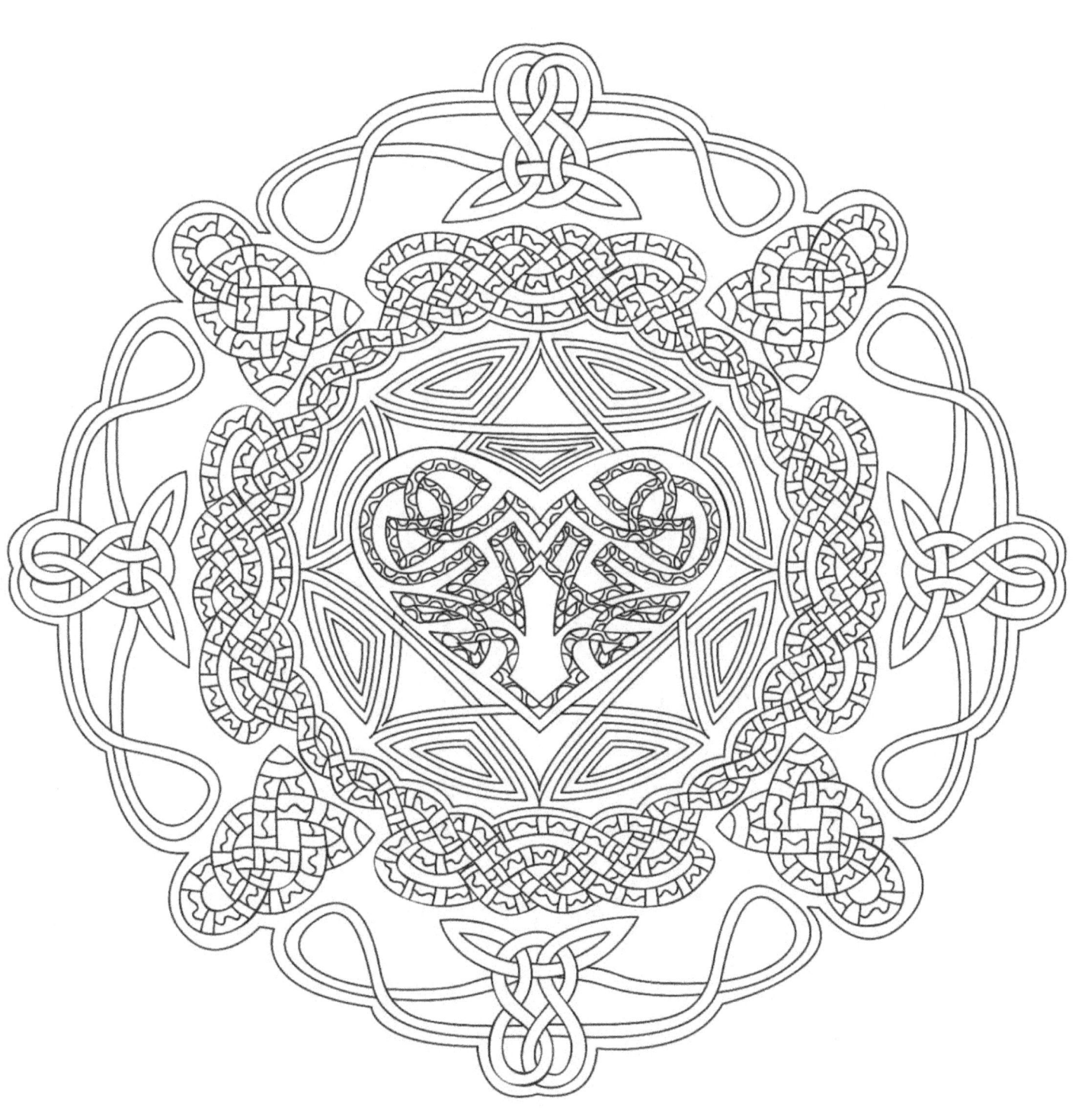

You Are Awesome! Regardless of what anyone else or even you think right now YOU are awesome!

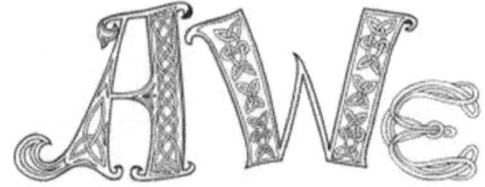

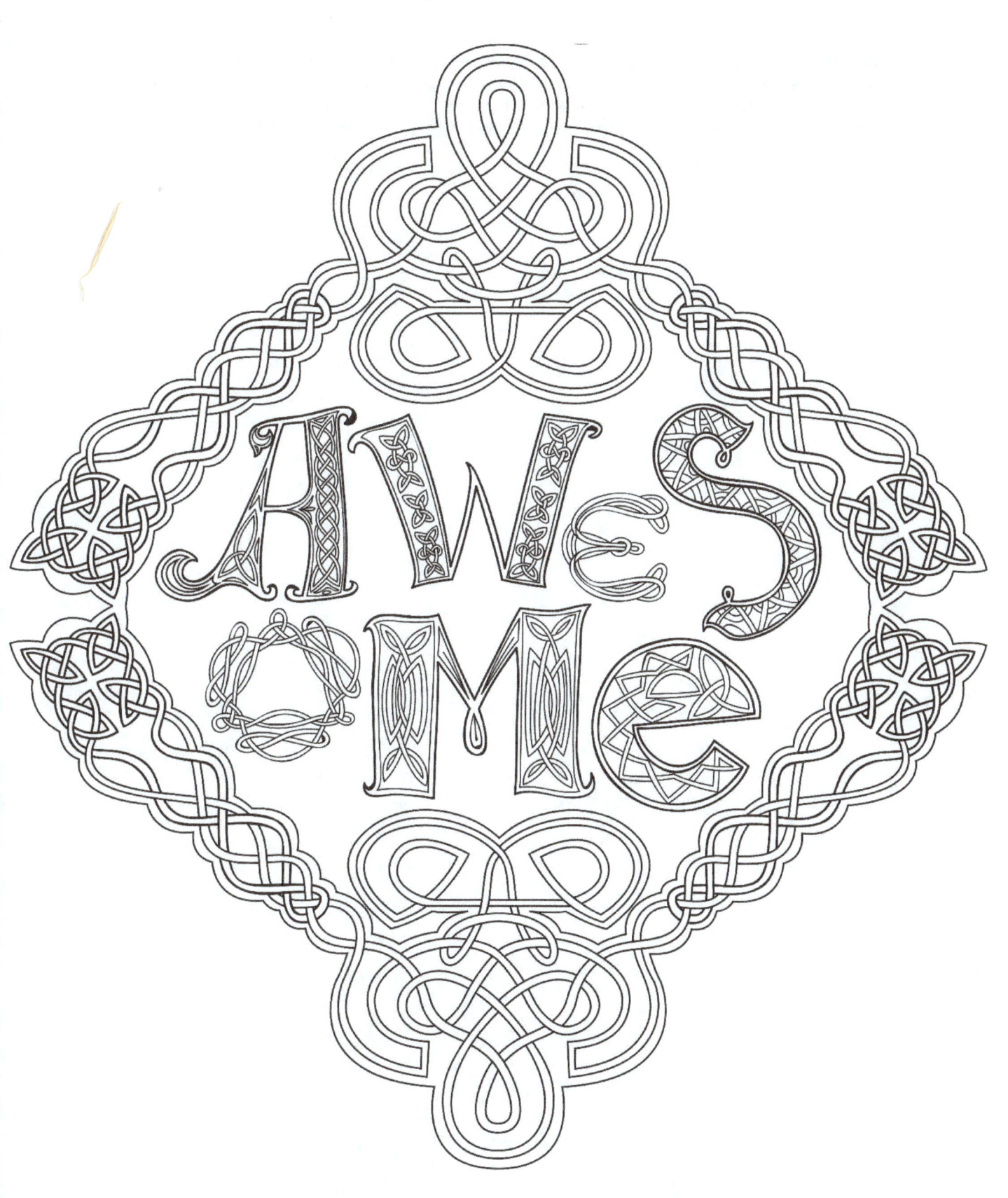

You Are Beautiful*:* There are lots of different kinds of beautiful and trust me, you are beautiful. If you're just not feeling it, take time every day to notice something beautiful about yourself. Take a moment to appreciate your eyes, your dimples, maybe the curve of your legs or your smile or your laugh.   If you make a point of looking for something you like about yourself every day, eventually you will learn to love yourself and see some of the beauty in you that other people already see.

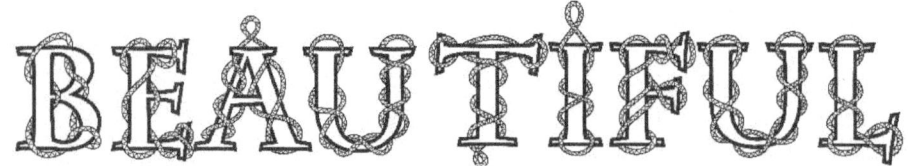

BEAU
TIFUL

You Are Worthy: You are just as good as anyone else on this Earth, so don't let others put you down. As Eleanor Roosevelt said, "No one can make you feel inferior without your consent." Do not give them your consent!

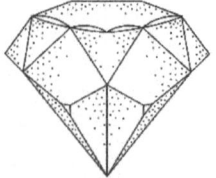

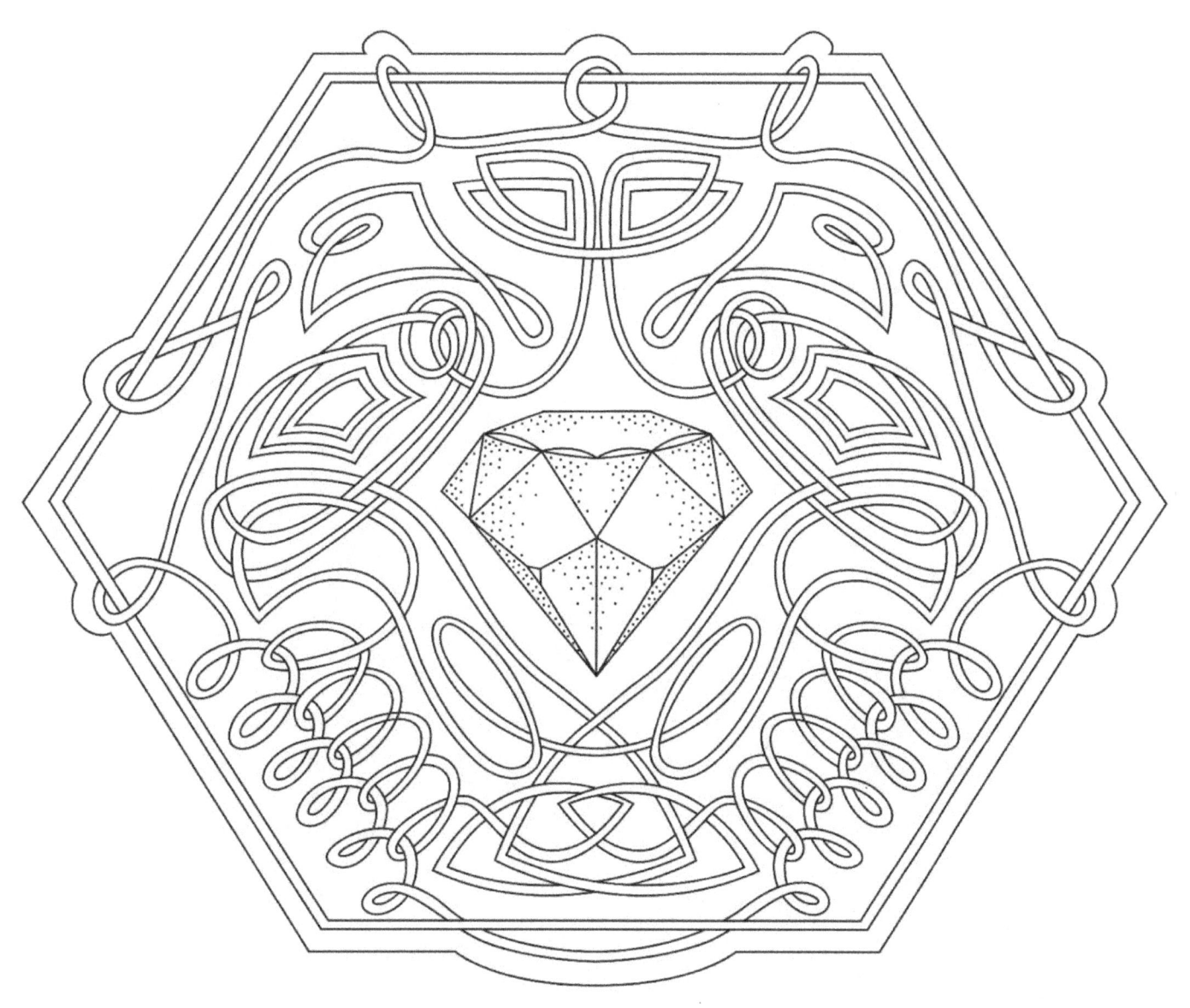

You Are Smart: Just like beauty, people are intelligent in different ways. My intelligence may be acedemic while yours might be fixing cars or knowing how to be at peak physical fitness or you can sing like a bird, but we're all smart at something. Recognize your own special intelligence, whatever it may be.

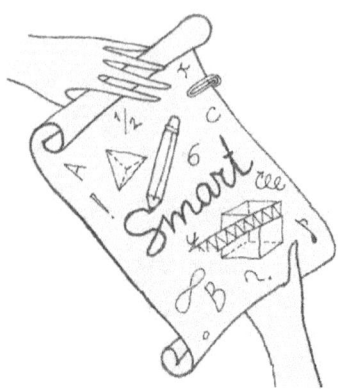

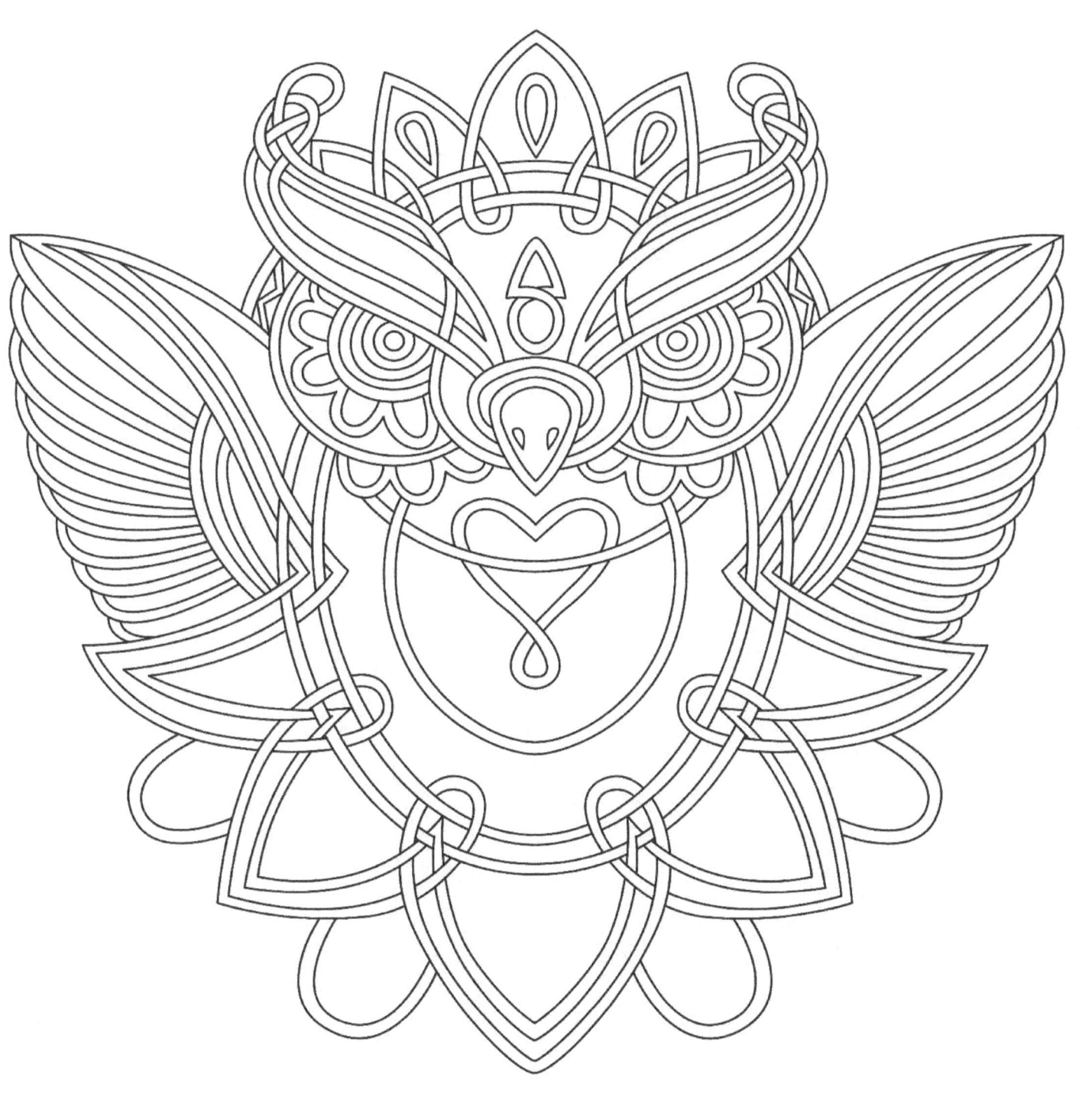

Be Proud Of Your Talents: Once you've recognized your unique super power, be proud of it! If someone is mean to you and picks on you because of what you are good at, just ignore them because they're probably just jealous that they aren't smart in the way that you are. Don't hide your abilities because of other people's insecurity or lack of understanding about it. Be happy and proud that you are so smart! Be happy and proud to be your awesome unique you.

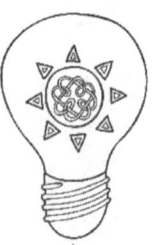

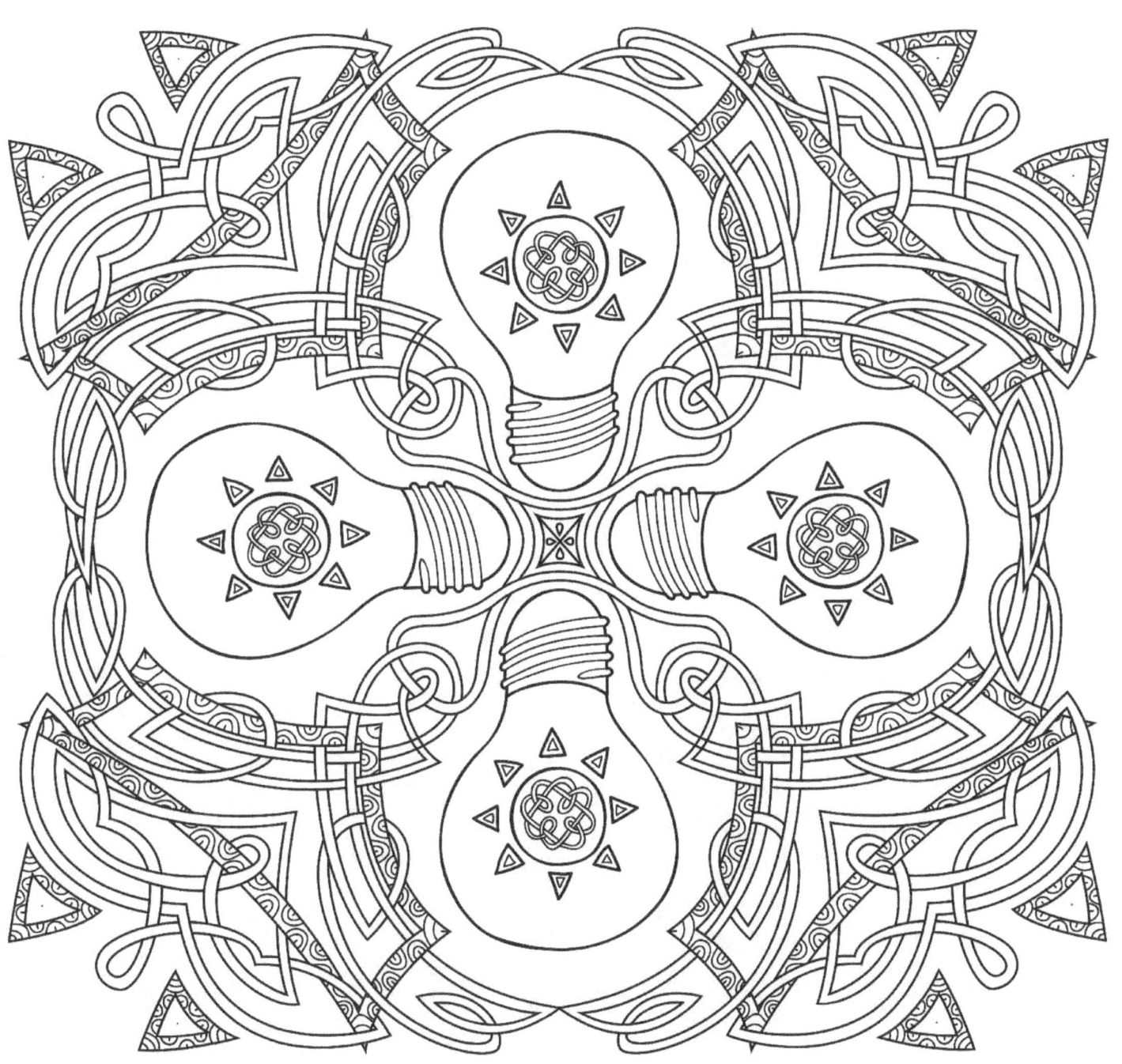

You are important: There will always be someone in whose life you are very important, even if you or they don't know it right now. You never know when the small kindness you do will have a big impact on another person's life so always strive to be kind and compassionate, even to yourself.

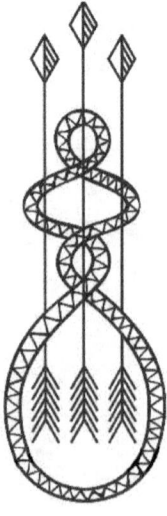

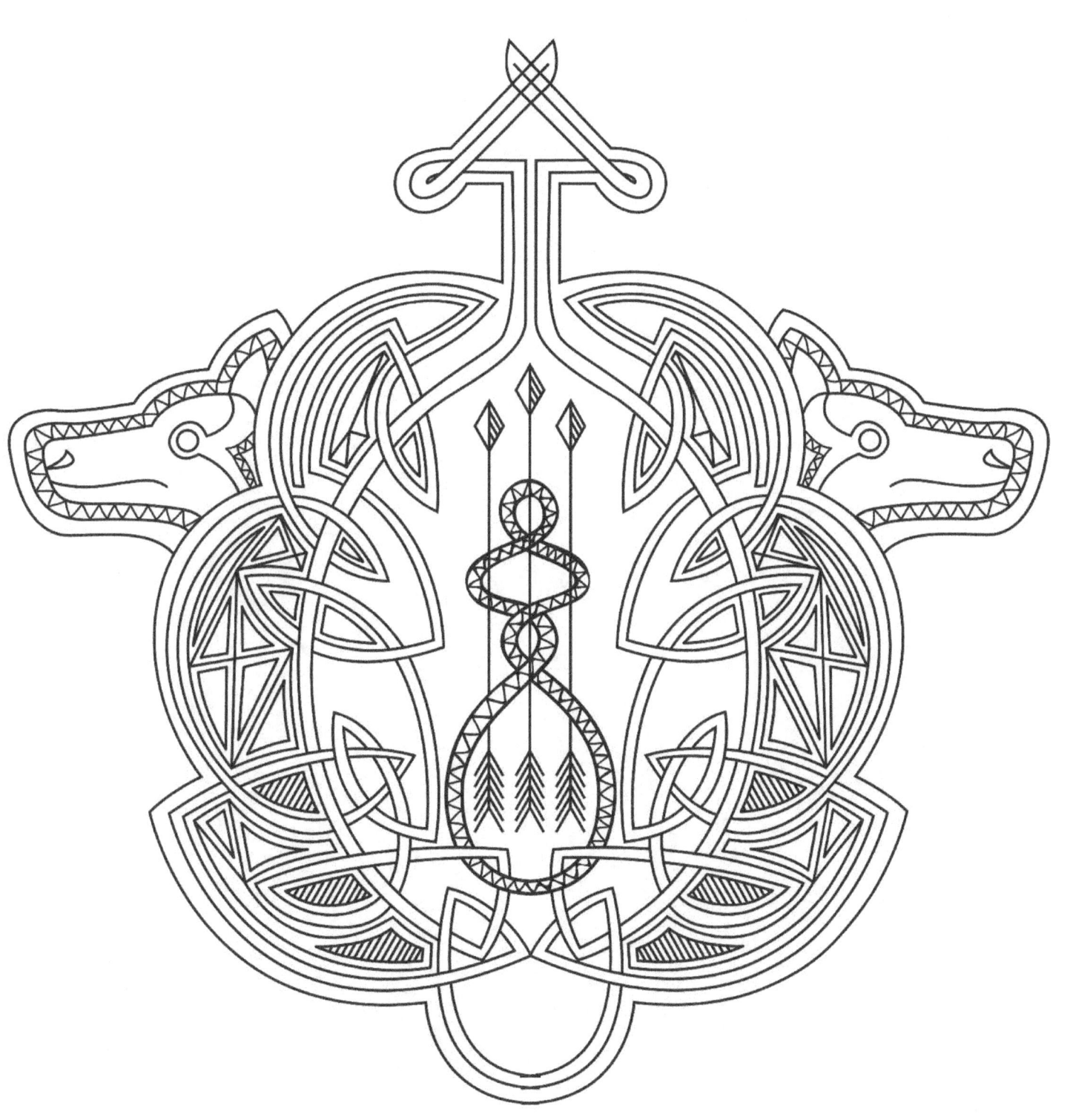

Respect Yourself: Your words and actions are a signal to other people about how you want to be treated. Be kind and respectful to yourself and others, and if people don't respect you in return, let them know that you deserve better. If they still don't get the idea, do you really want them in your life?

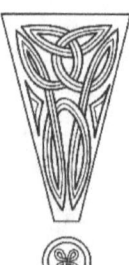

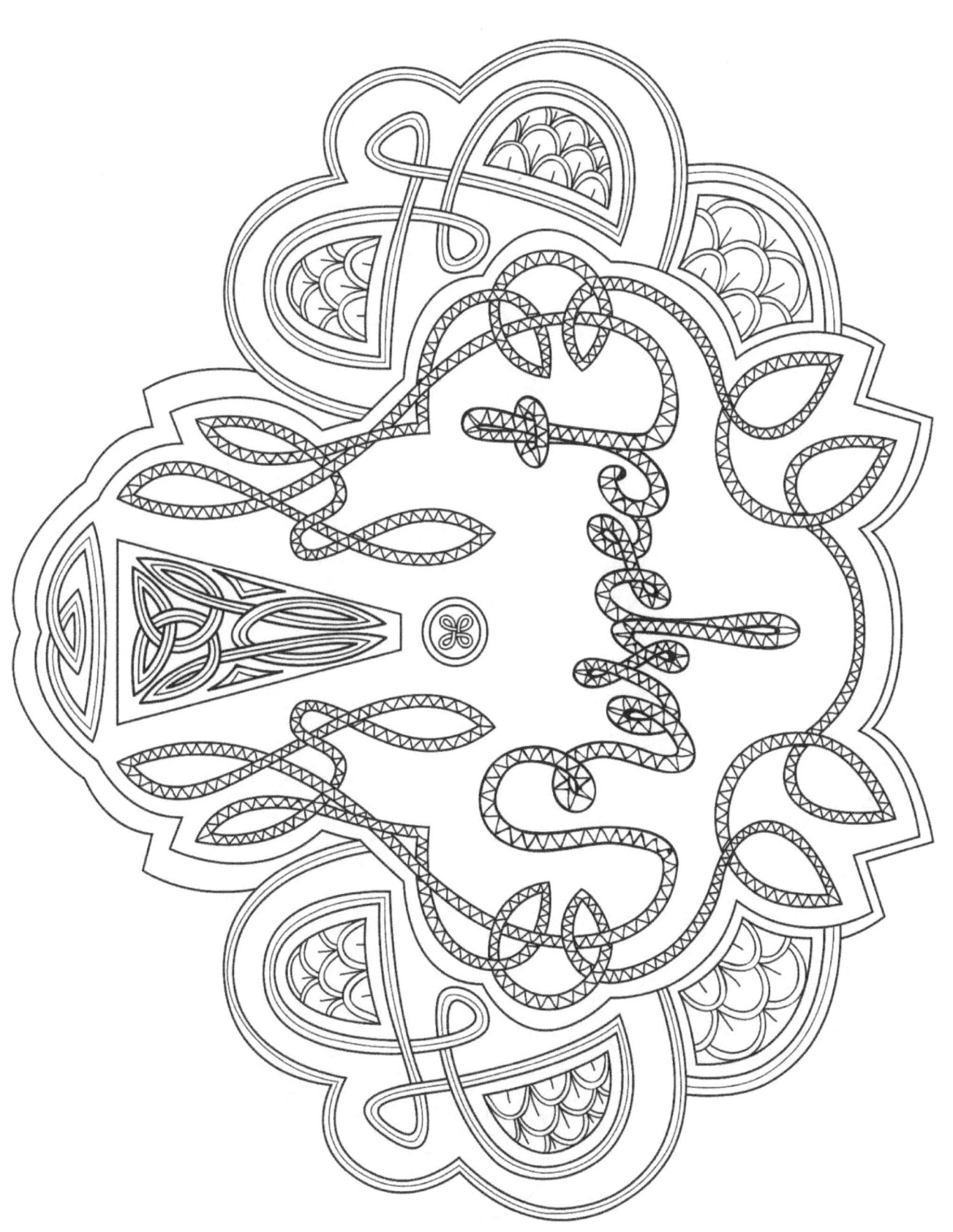

Your Life Makes A Difference: There is only one person with your unique skills, personality and abilities. No one else can fill your role in this world. Your life makes a difference.

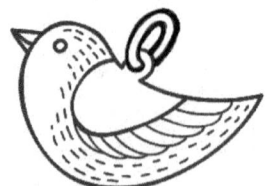

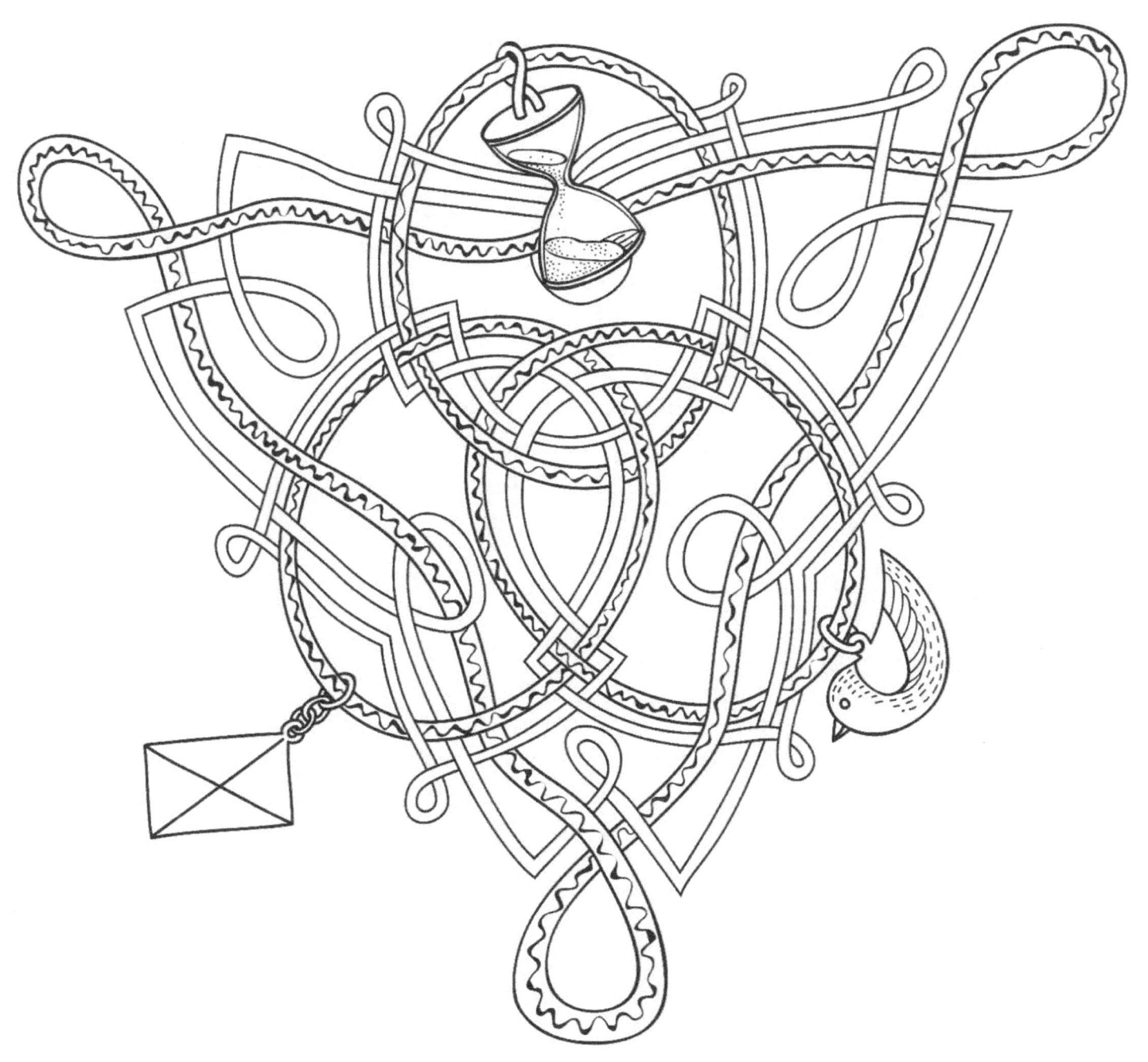

Ignore Mean People: Feeling empathy and kindness toward others does not mean letting them walk all over you. You need to guard your heart against mean people. Know that their attitude is a reflection of something in themselves that they don't like, and not you. If you let them be mean to you, they may think it is acceptable. Respect that they are on a different life path than you with different lessons to learn, but if they're mean, sometimes it's best to just walk away and let it go.

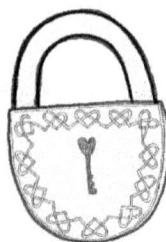

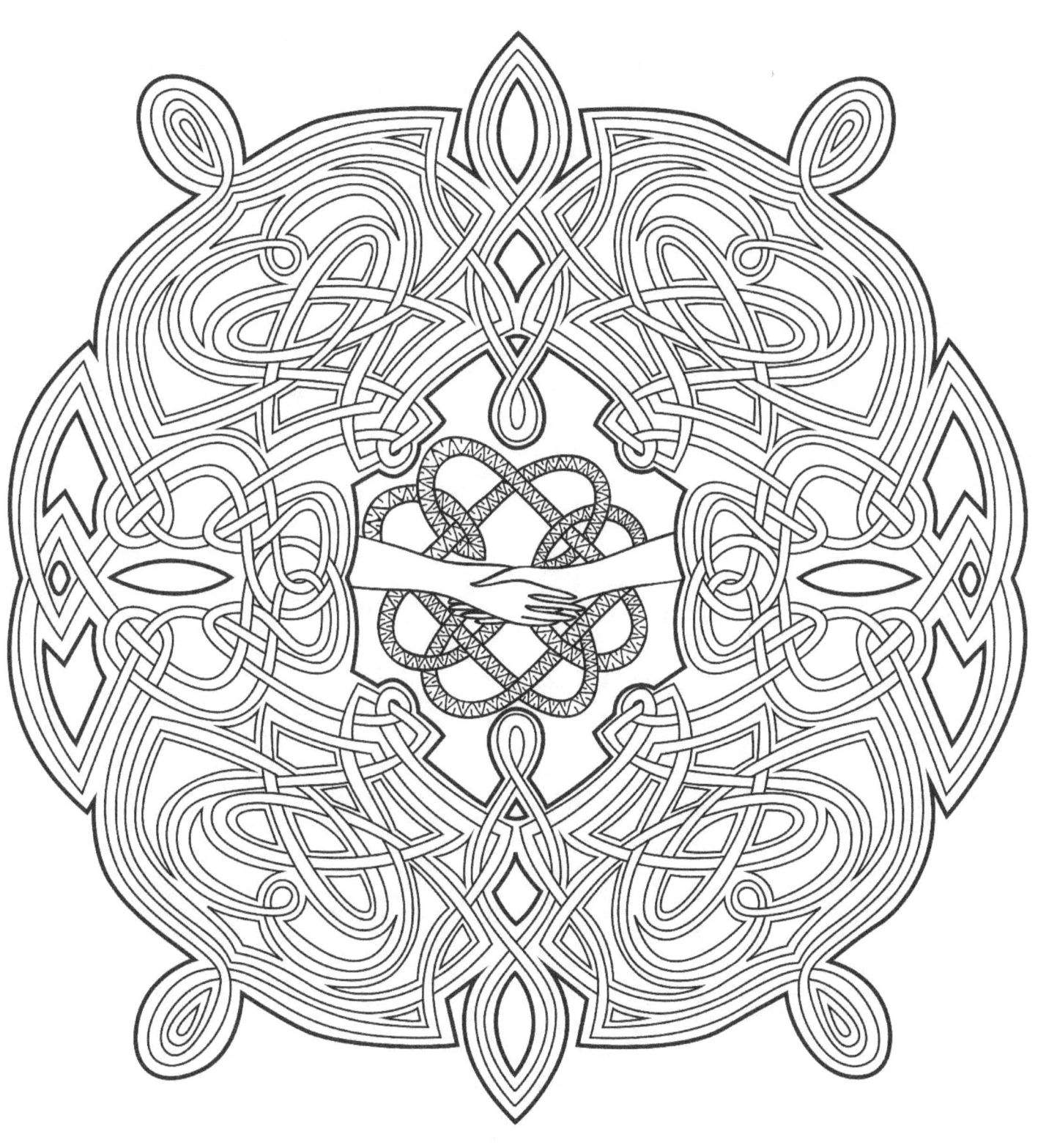

Always Be Kind: Try not to judge people. Often when they're behaving in an unacceptable way it's because they are hurting somehow or confused. You don't know what their path is or what they're going through so treat them with empathy. The Dali Lama said, "Be kind whenever possible. It is always possible."

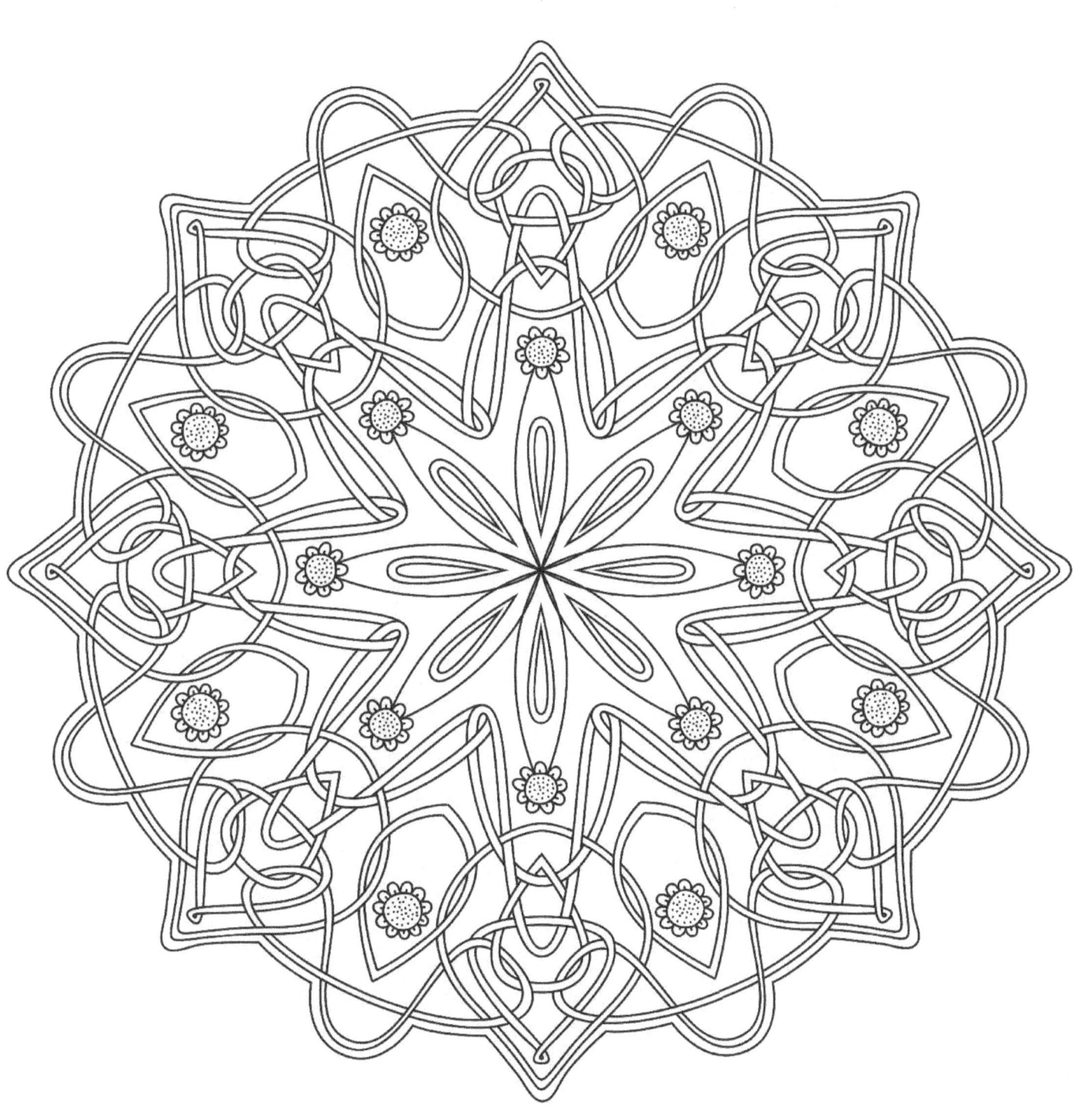

Confidence Is Attractive: People are naturally drawn to confident, happy people. If you're not particularly feeling that way, try making yourself smile. I do this and it helps me to feel better when things are bad. Acting confident and happy makes you feel more that way, and it becomes a habit. Before you know it your whole world can be looking better.

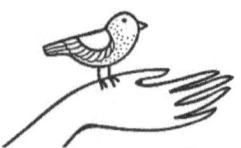

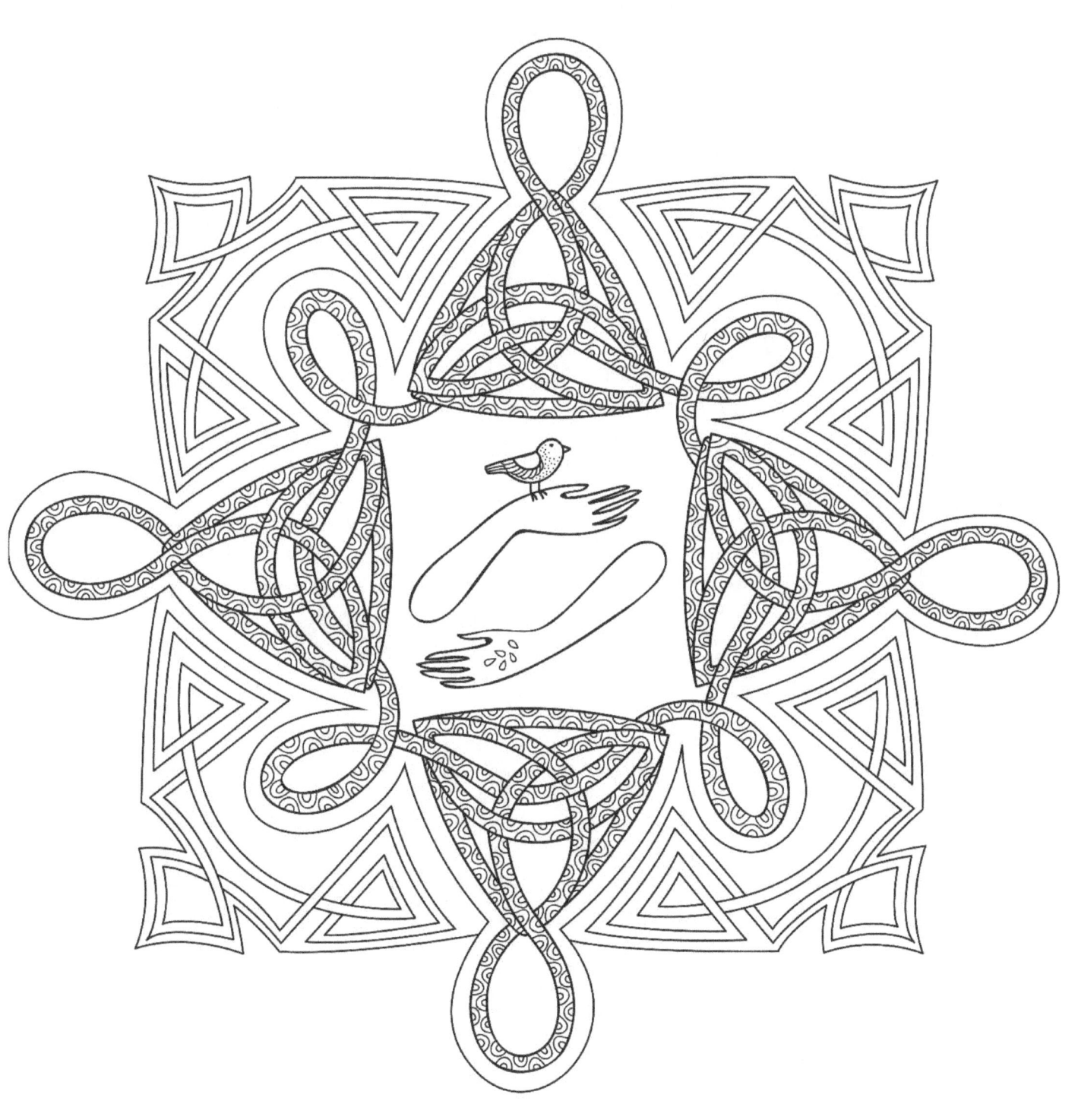

The World Isn't Always Fair: When our love leaves us or we get fired from a job for no fault of our own, or get blamed for something we didn't do we may say, "It's just not fair!" Learn to accept the things you can't change and look for the good in everything. It will help you feel better. Remember too that when one door closes we suddenly notice others that are open. Relax, be calm, and know that better things are coming.

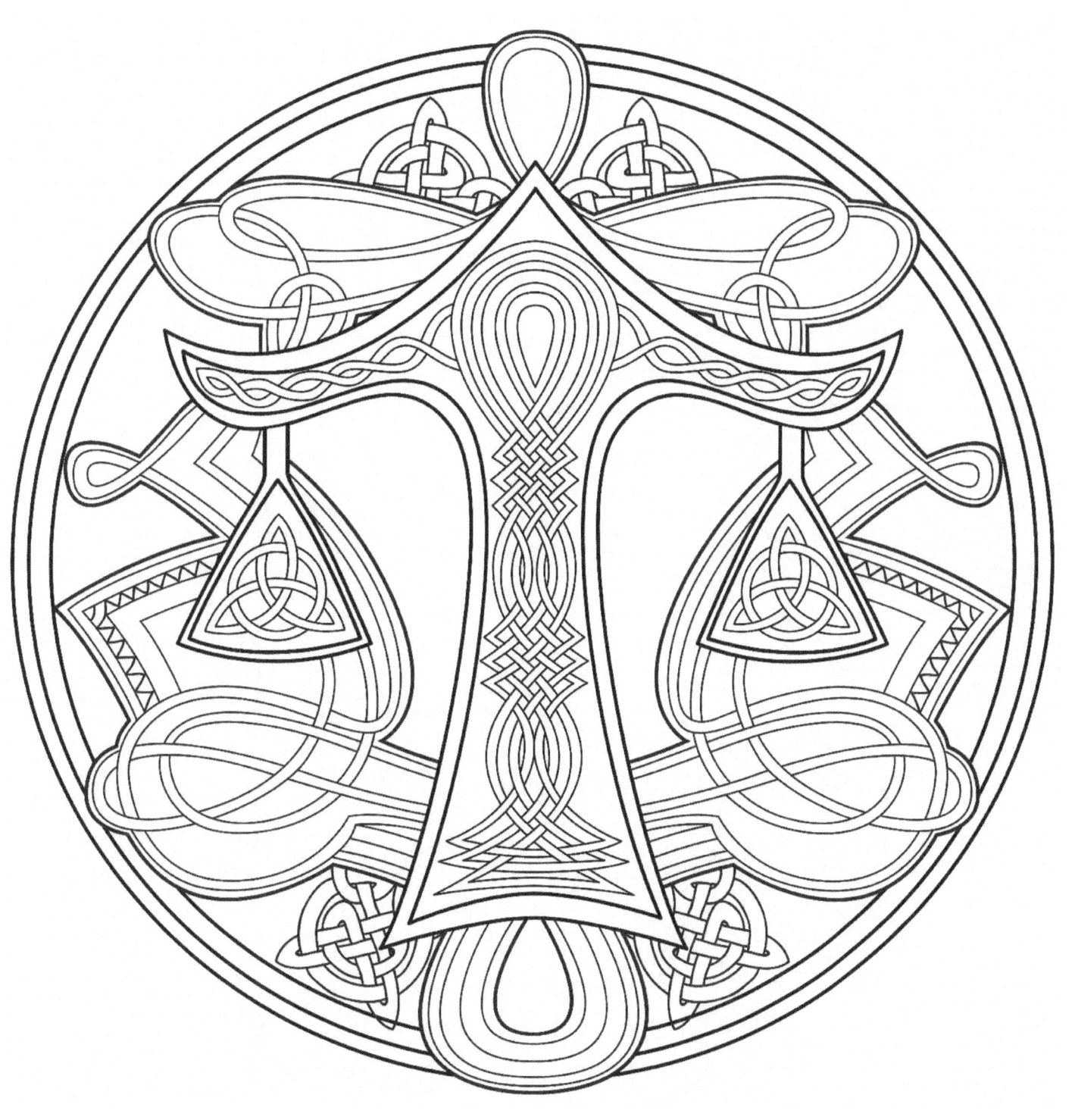

Everyone Is Different: Don't worry if you can't do something that someone else can. There are probably skills you have that they don't. The fact that we're all different is awesome because it means that together we can accomplish far more than we could alone.

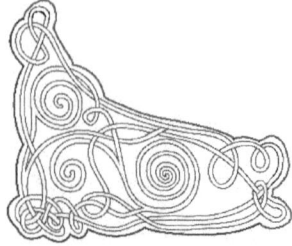

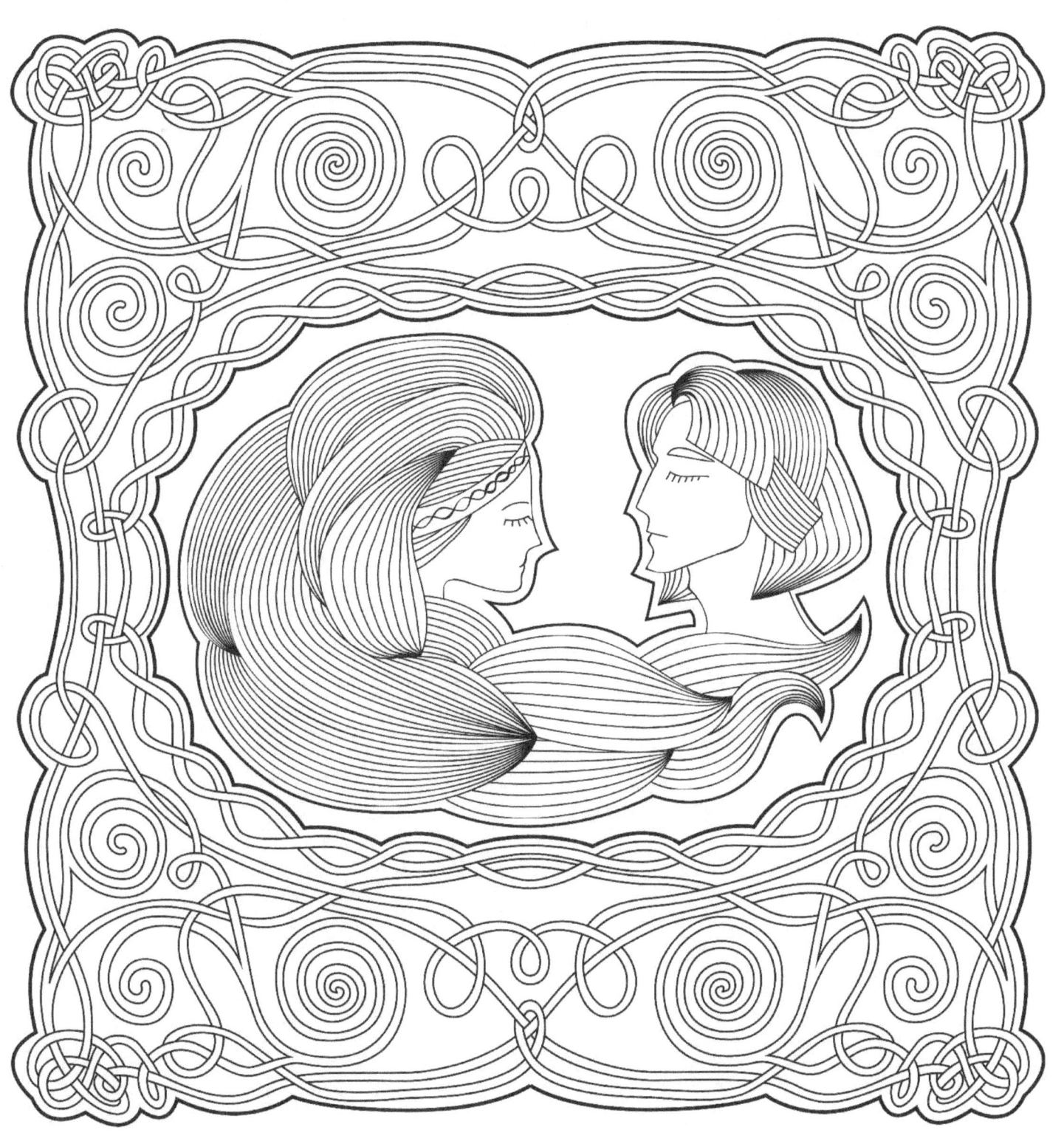

Don't Lose Yourself: When we're in relationships we generally want to please the other person. This is good, but remember who you were and keep doing those things and tending those friendships that you had before you became a couple. Don't become someone else to please anyone. You and your relationship will be healthier that way.

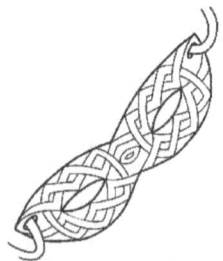

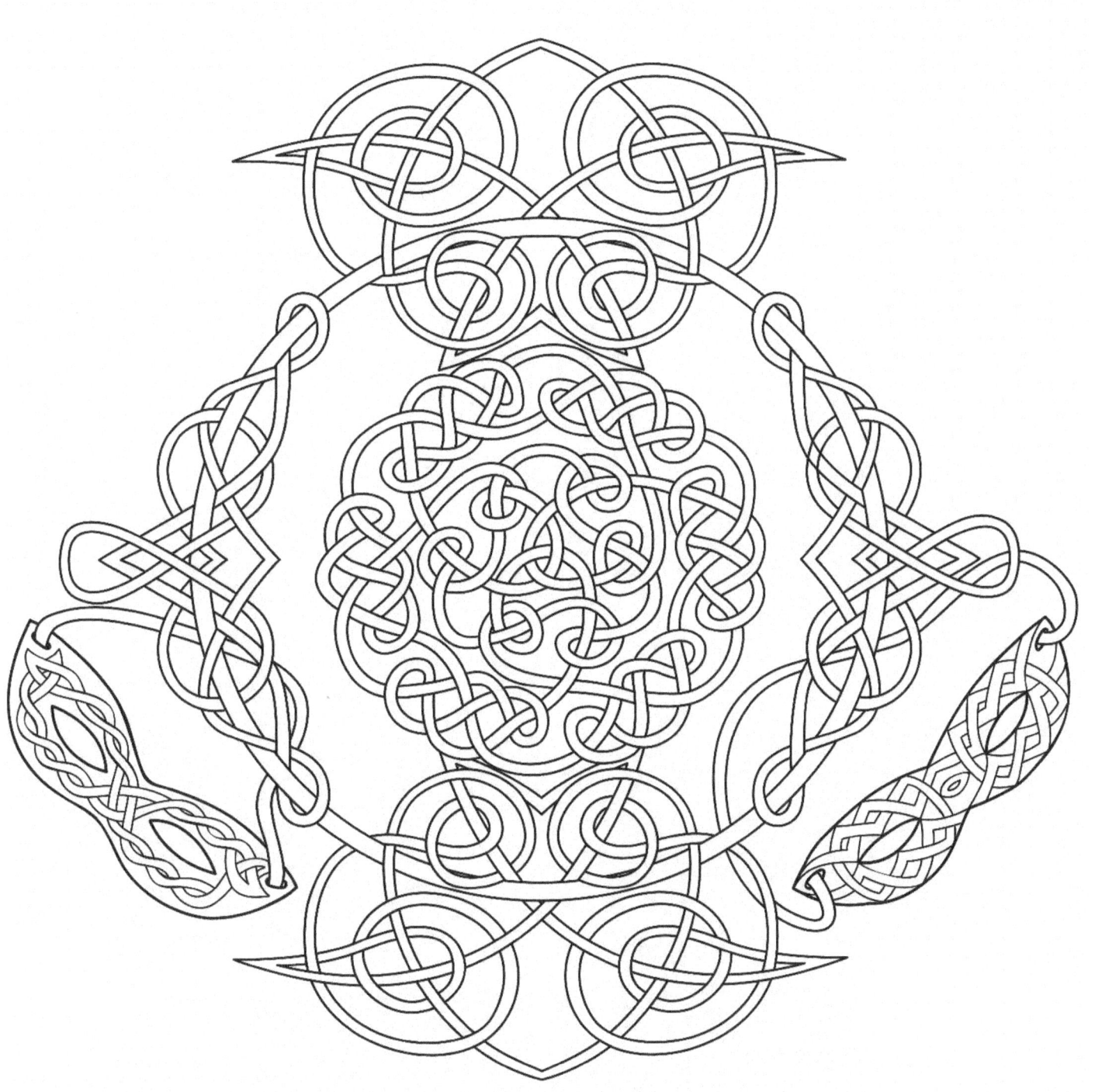

Take Care of Yourself: Many of us are nurturing people and this is good, but you have to remember to take care of yourself too. You need time to take care of your own health, wealth, and happiness so that you'll be able to share with others. When you think of it that way, taking care of yourself is not being selfish. It is being more generous.

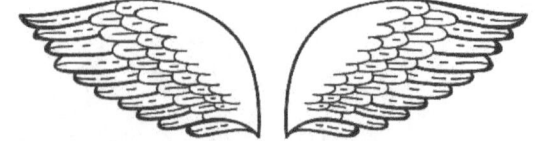

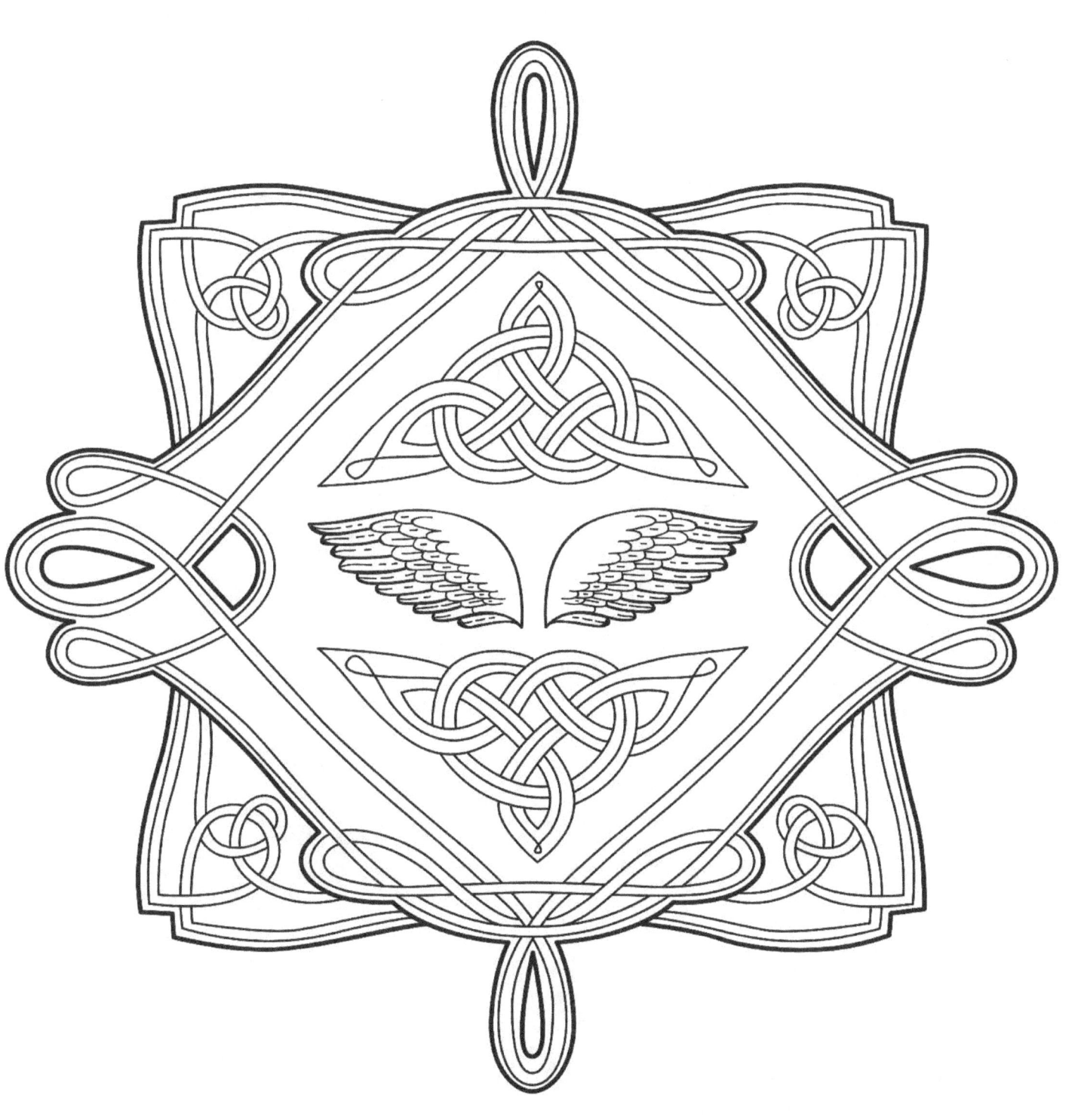

Goals: It's important to set goals to give yourself a direction. If you're not sure just pick one, and start going. You need to take actions to move in the direction of your goals. Even small actions count. You can change course later if you decide to, but be going *somewhere*. Choose your life. Don't let someone else or circumstance choose for you.

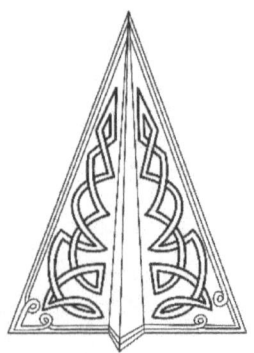

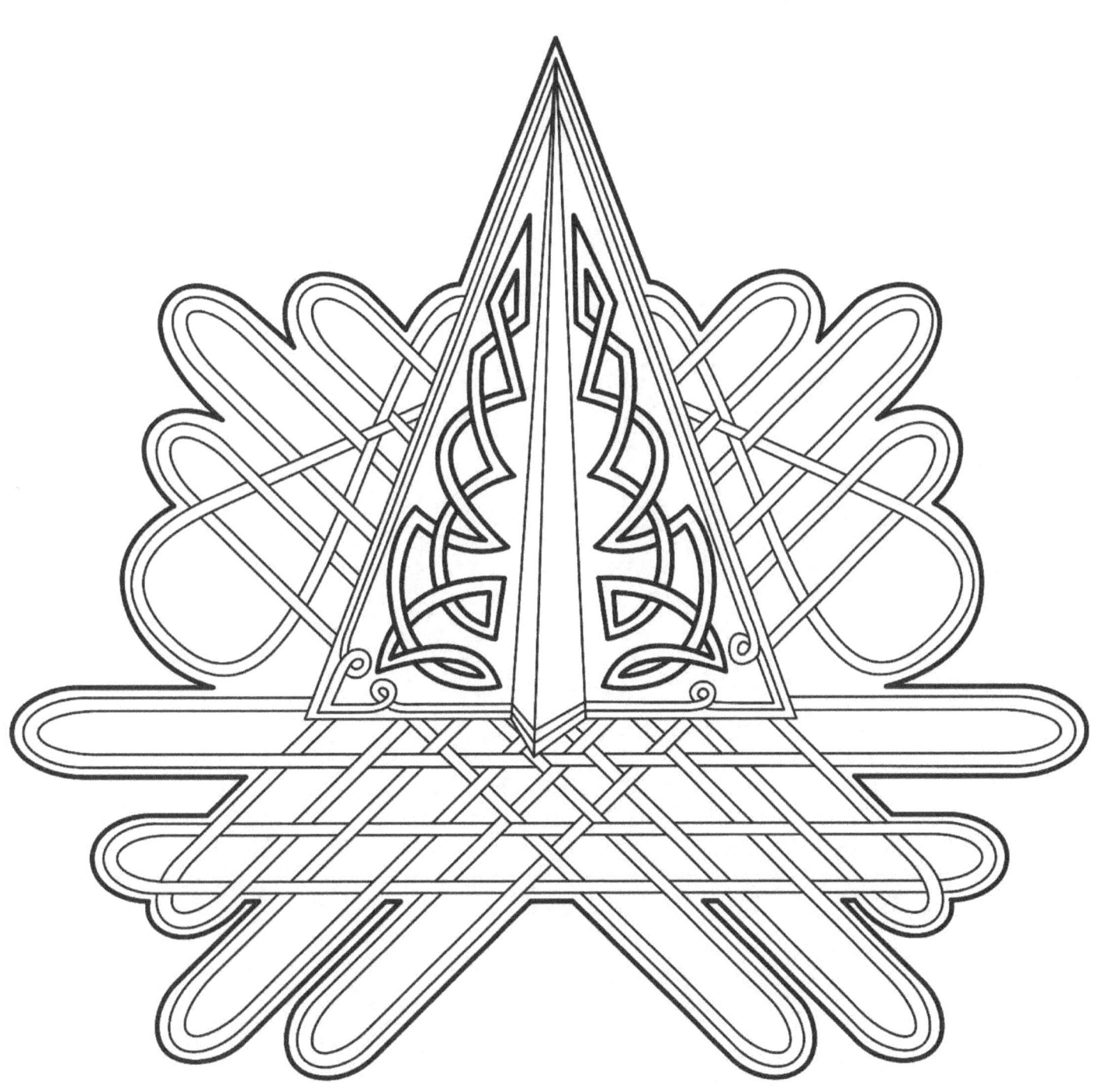

You Can Achieve Anything: When you make up your mind that you want something, write it down. Think about it before you go to sleep, and even while you're sleeping your brain will work on how to get what you want. Be positive in your ability to achieve your goal and keep taking steps in that direction. As Lao Tzu said, "The journey of a thousand miles begins with a single step."

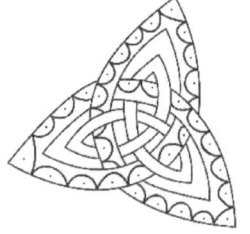

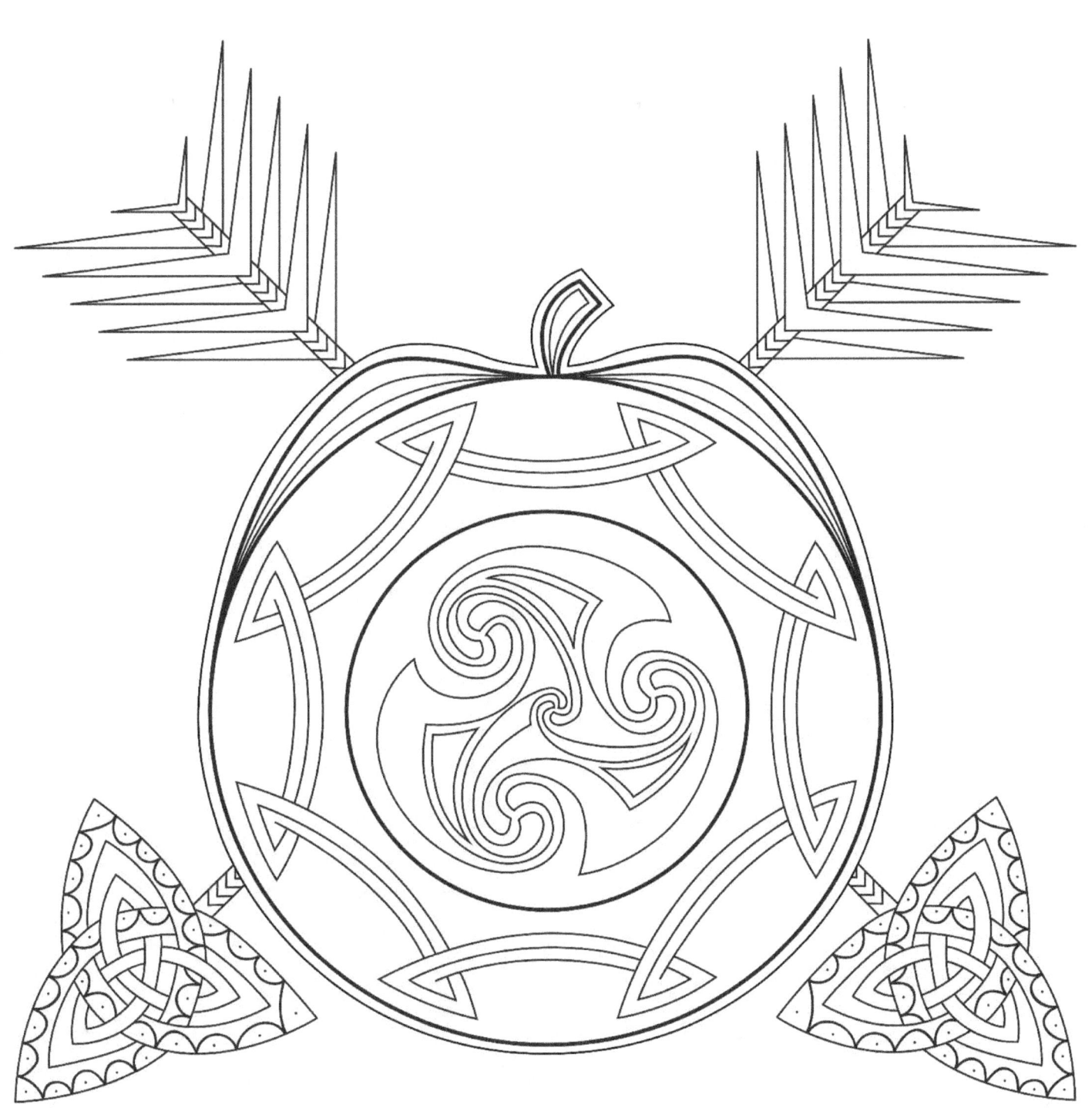

Tune Out Negativity: Choose to be happy. Tune out other people's negative talk and vibes. Happiness is a choice and everything in life seems easier when you're feeling happy. If you feel sad, smile. Trust me, it helps!

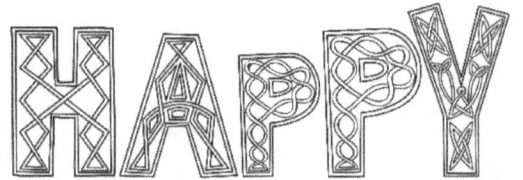

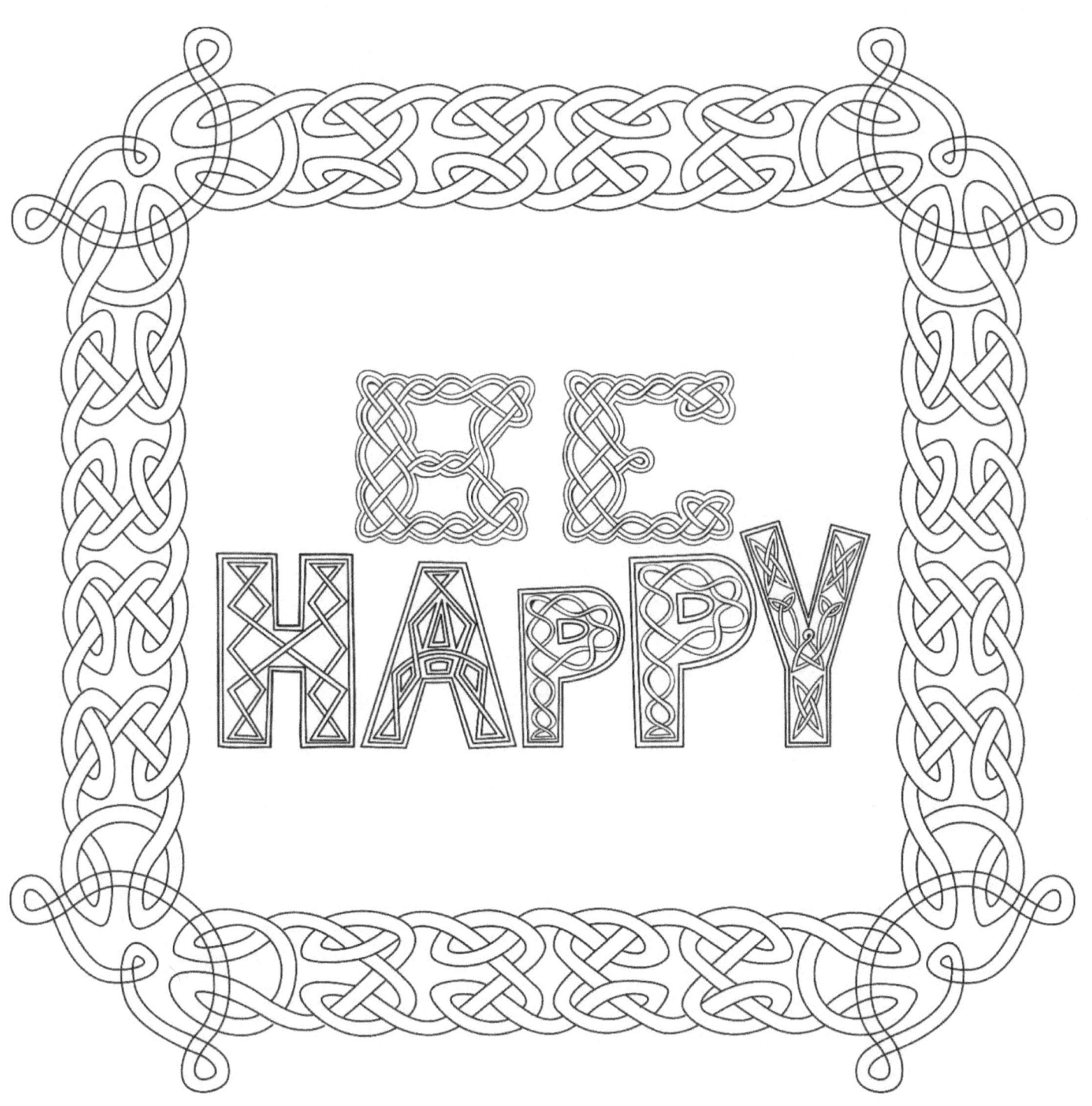

Be Careful of the Company You Keep: Surround yourself with people who believe in you and will support you in your dreams. Don't let a "Debbie downer" destroy your momentum. Spend time with people who have achieved or want to achieve the same sort of things that you do. They can be good inspirations and full of ideas and positive input.

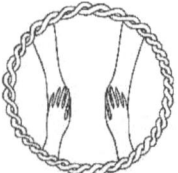

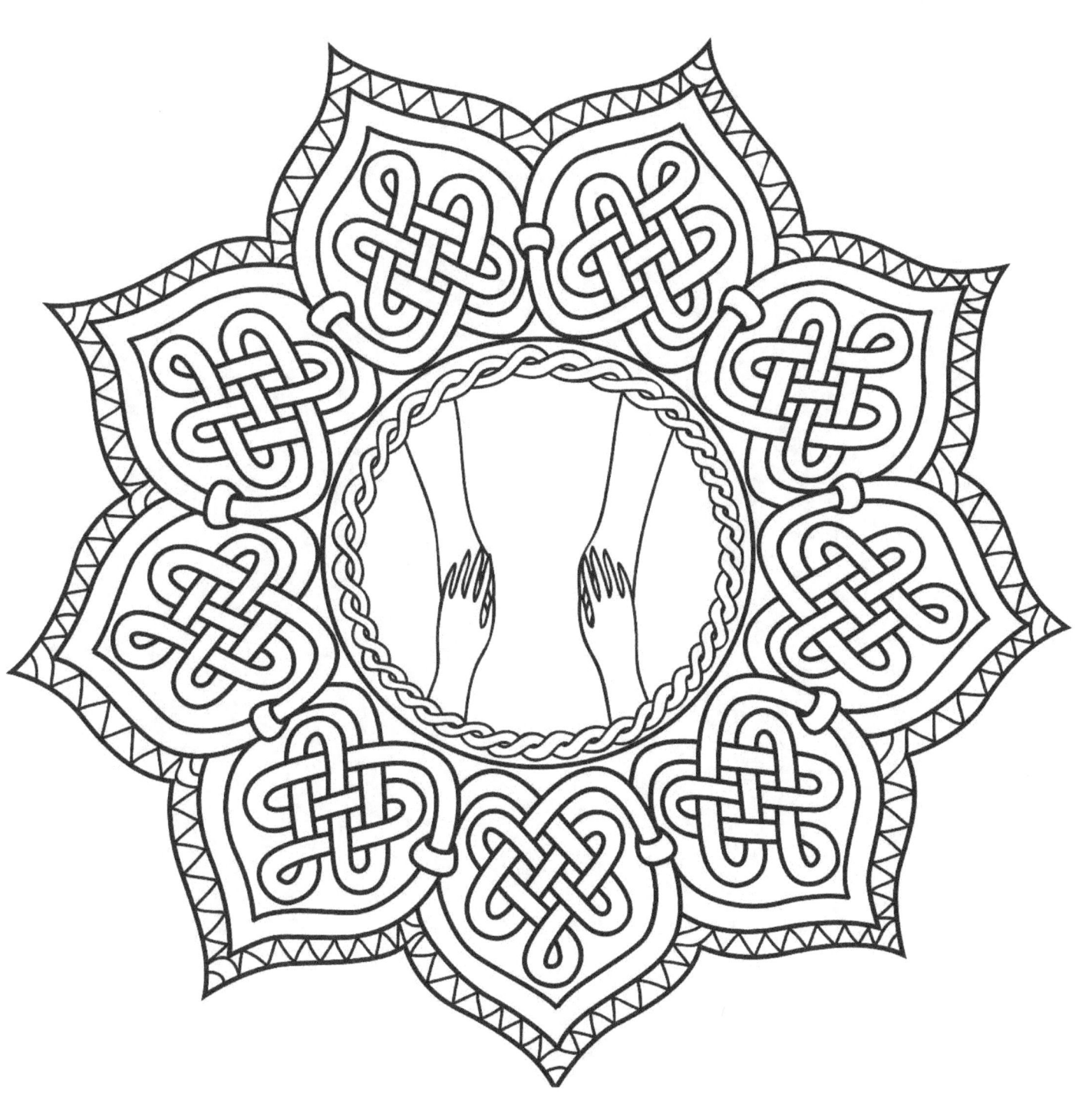

Believe In Yourself! Believe in your own ability to get things done. Believe in yourself to achieve great things. When you tell yourself you can, you open up and notice things that will help you. When you say, "I can't" or "I'll try" instead of "I will", it instills negativity that will sabotage your plans. Believing in yourself is your first step to achieving your dreams.

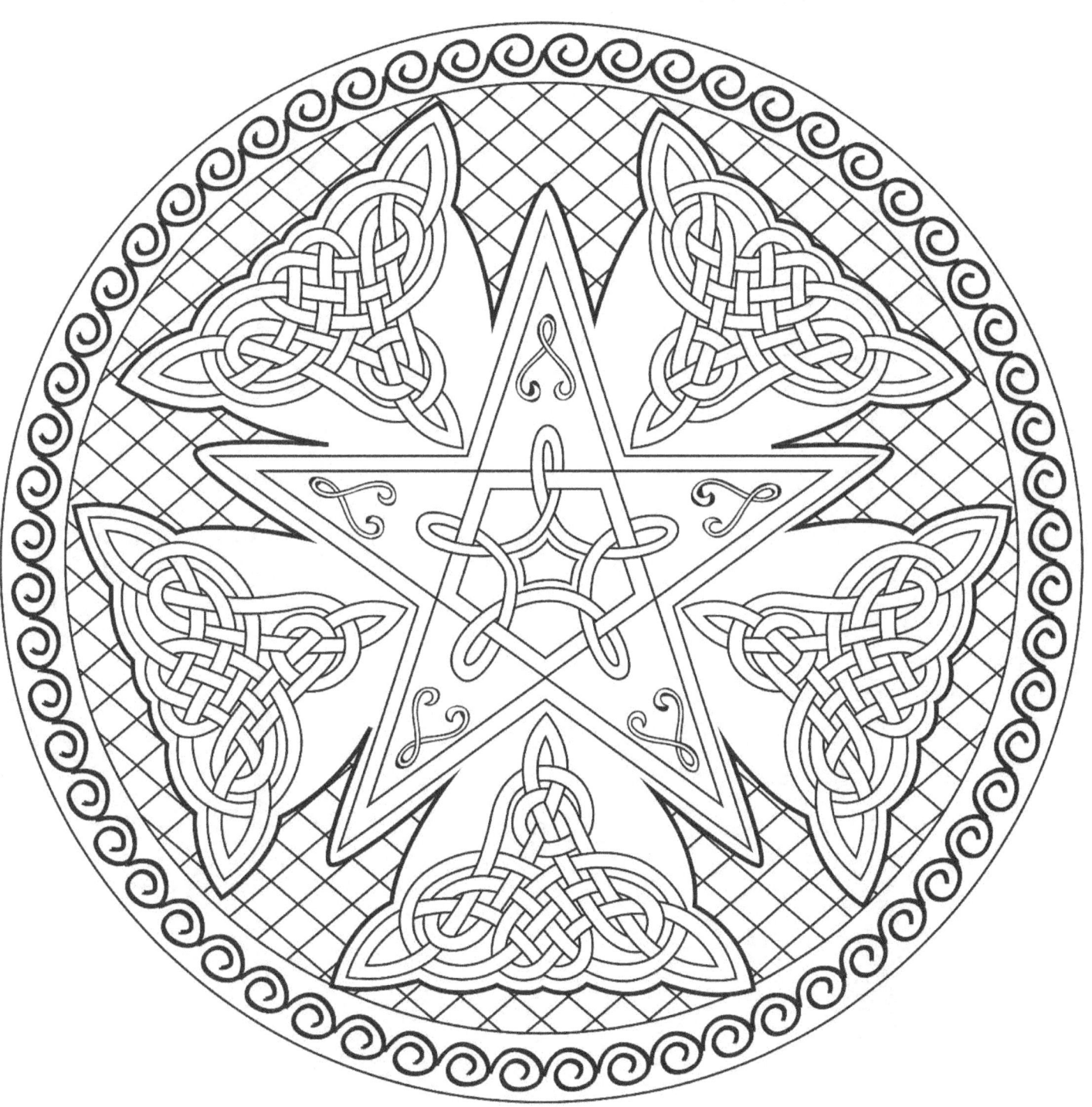

Be Responsible for Your Lfe: Be responsible for your own life. Make your own choices, or you'll have to live with the choices other people make for you and you may not like them! Remember that you always have a choice. You might not like your options but it is up to you to choose.

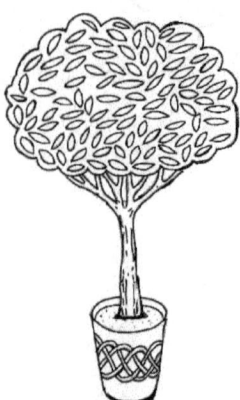

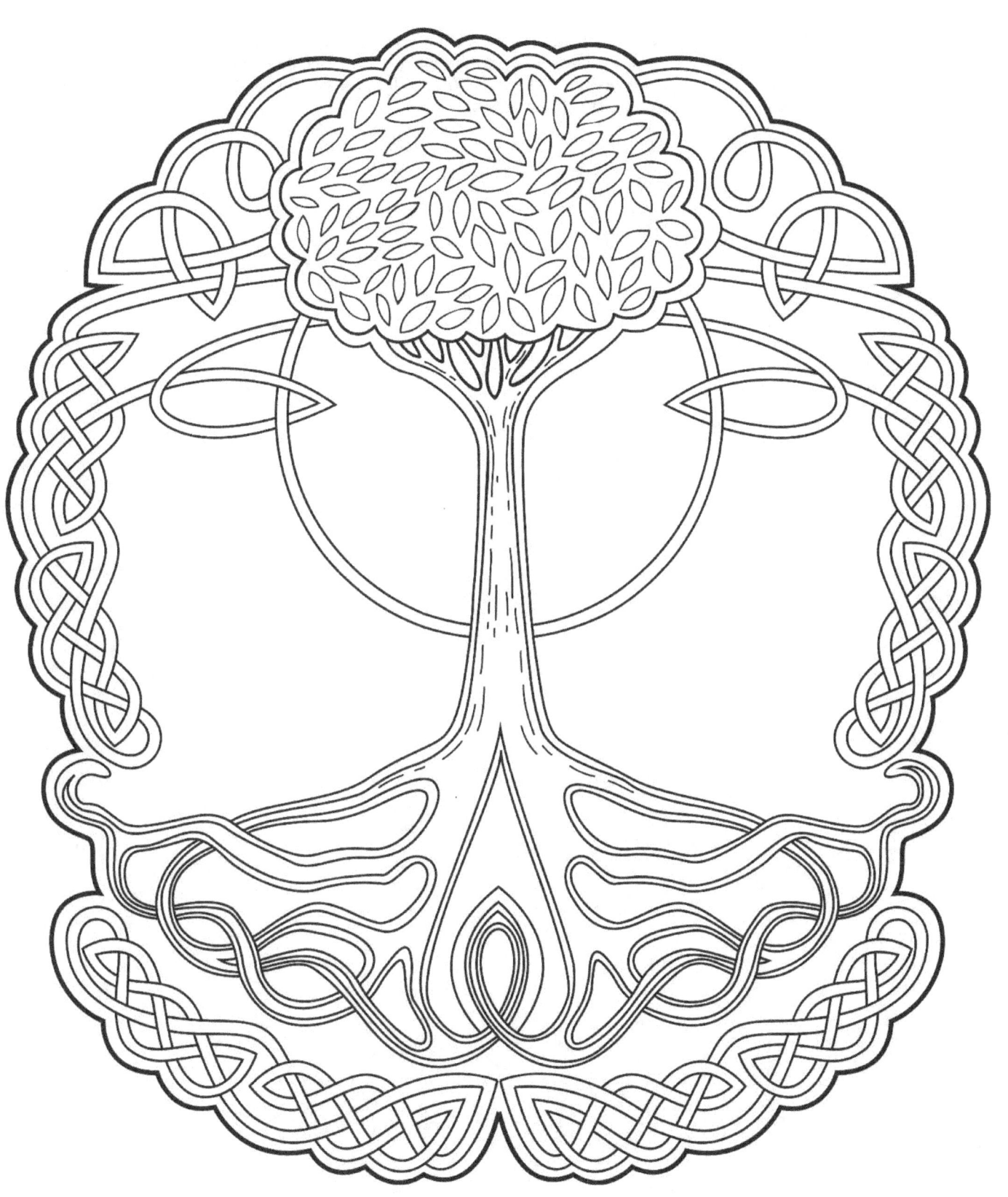

Focus on Your Goals: Having goals is great, but life offers so very many ways to get distracted from them. Do something that will remind you of your goals daily so that you will do something every day to reach those goals. Set an alarm on your phone or put a post-it on your refrigerator that says, "What did you do today to reach your goals?" Focus on your goals, keep taking action in that direction, and they will become reality.

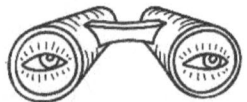

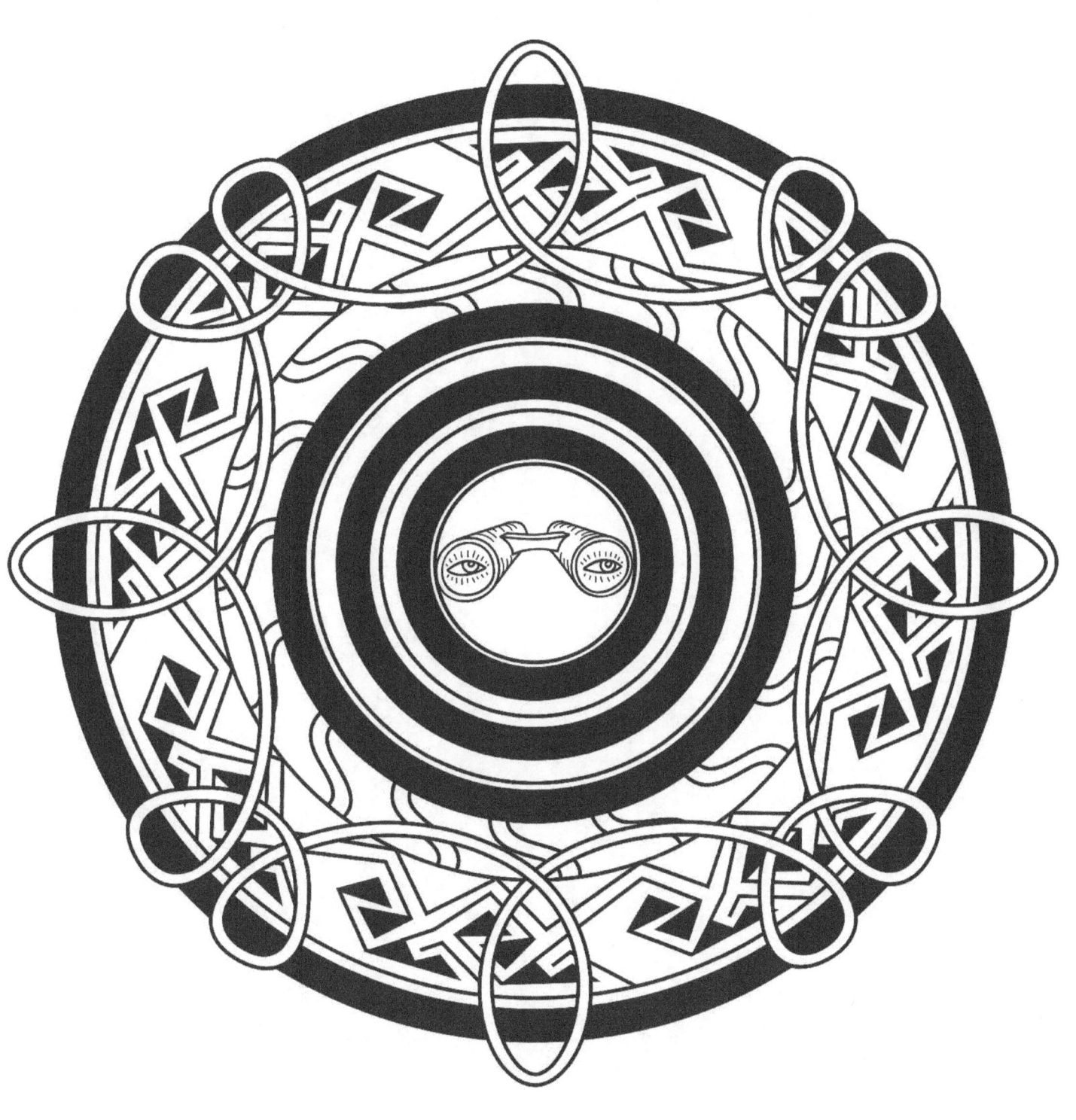

Be Tenacious! Sometimes "no" just means that you need to change the question or the approach. Consider a temporary failure to be education. Learn, adapt your approach and keep going until you succeed.

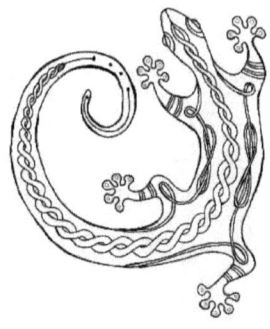

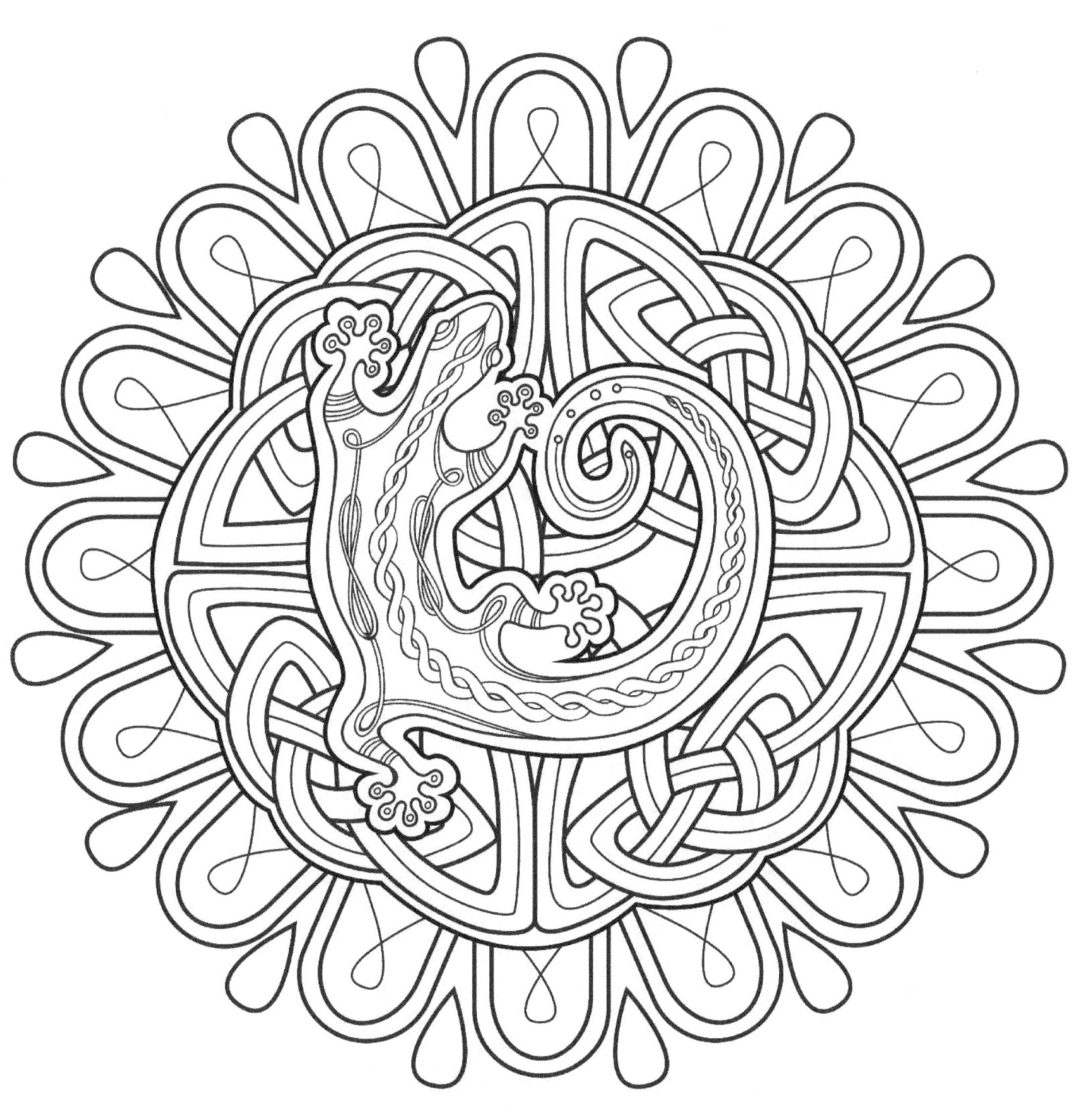

Always Have a Backup Plan: It's important to have a goal that you're focused on, but it's also important to have a backup plan. Have savings or a skill to cover the "what if" and to get you through those temporary failures until you reach your goal.

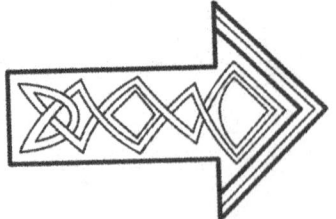

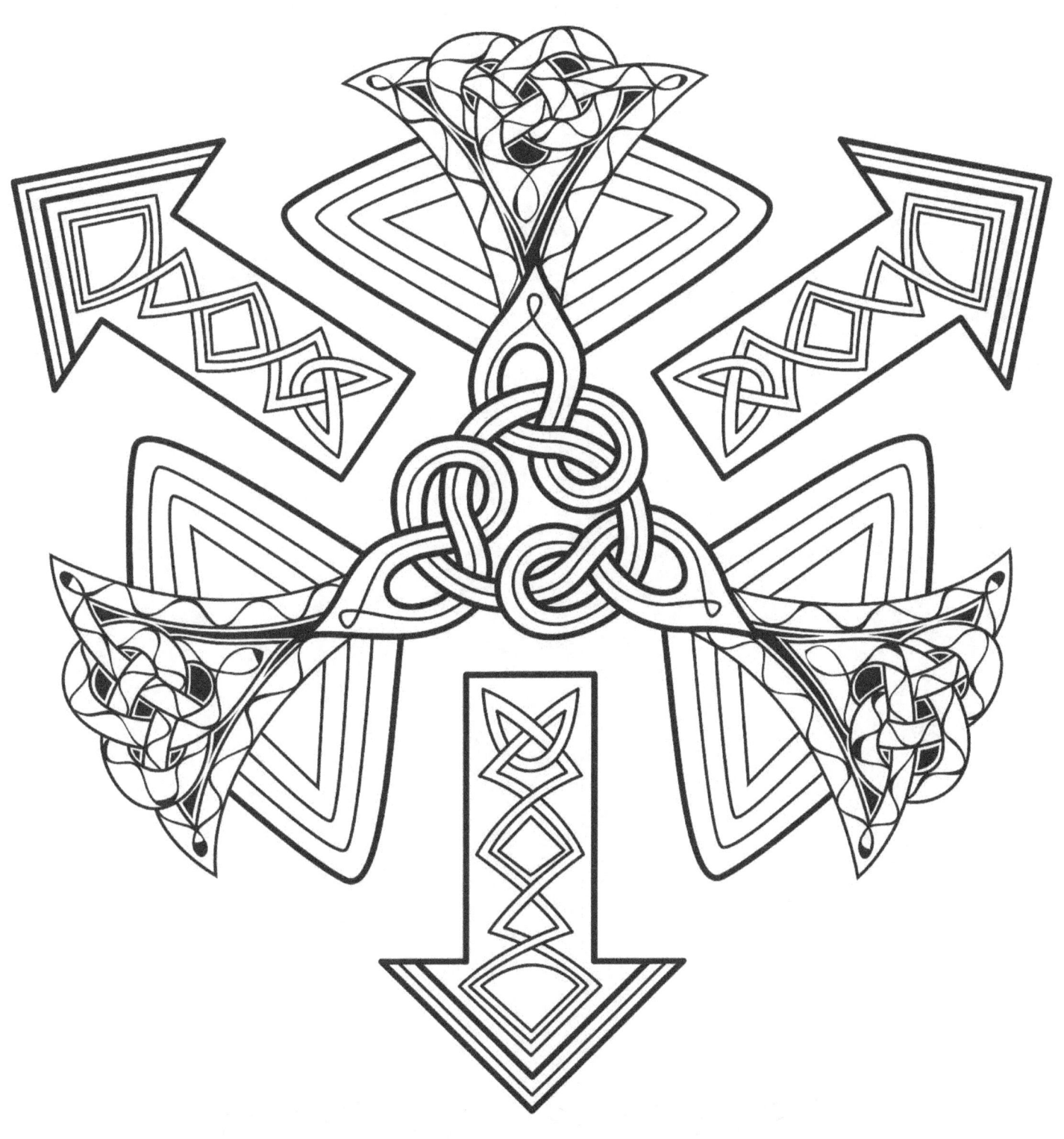

Money is Not Evil: Money might not be able to buy happiness, but it can make your life much easier. It's just a tool to get the things you need to help yourself and others. Money is your friend. Respect it and put it to good use.

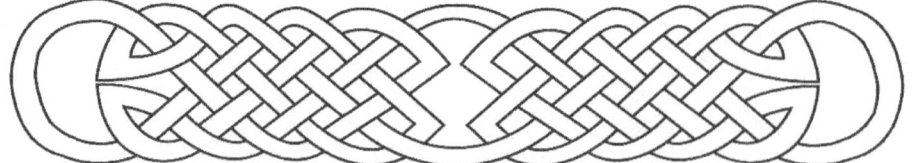

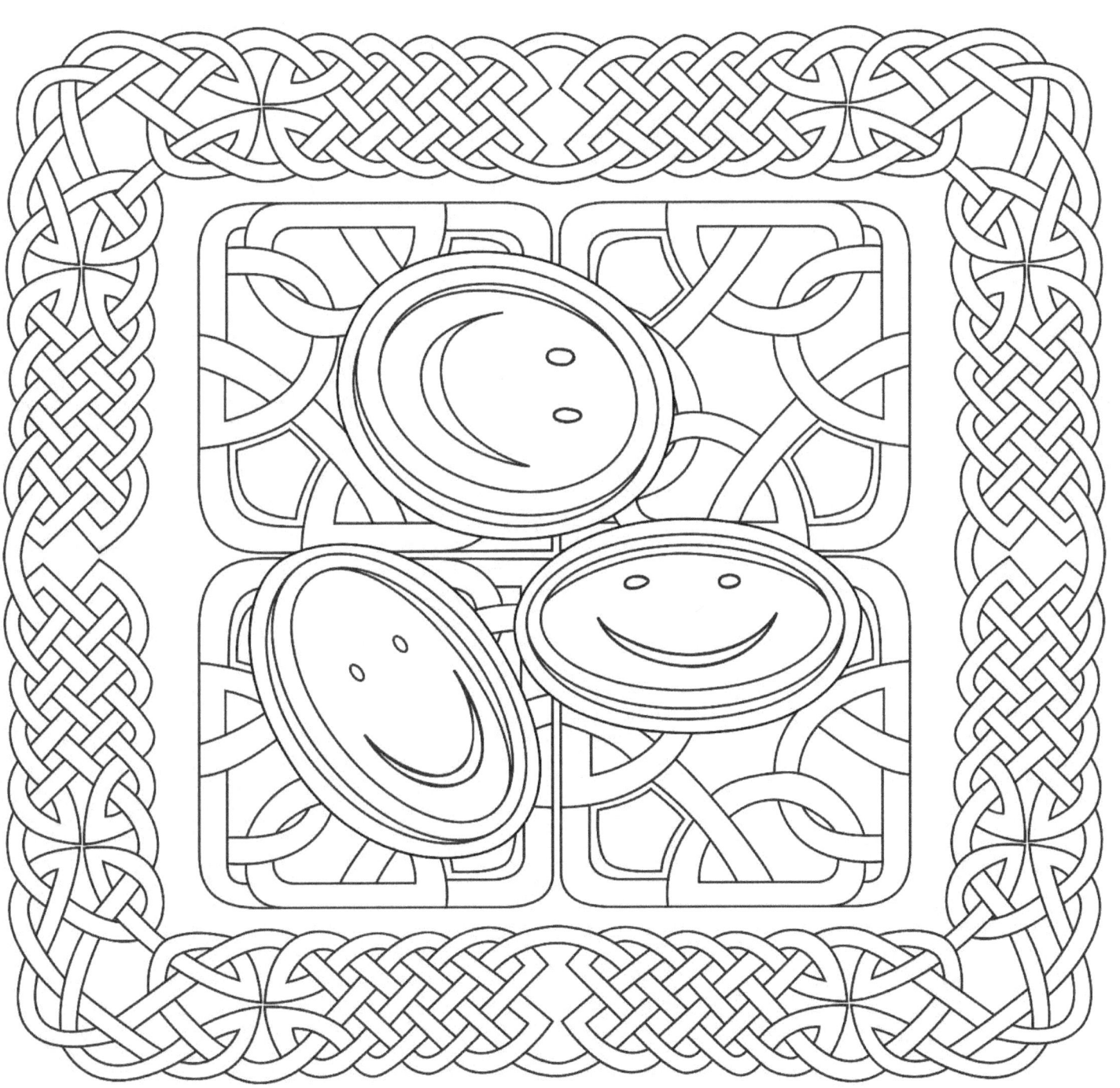

Have Some Money of Your Own: It's important. Money gives you choices, whether it's to get a ride home and get out of a bad situation, or to start a business. You need to have power over your own life, and money *is* power.

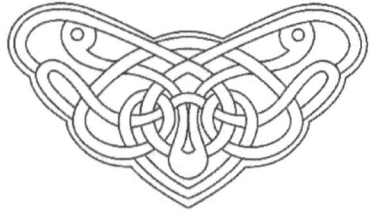

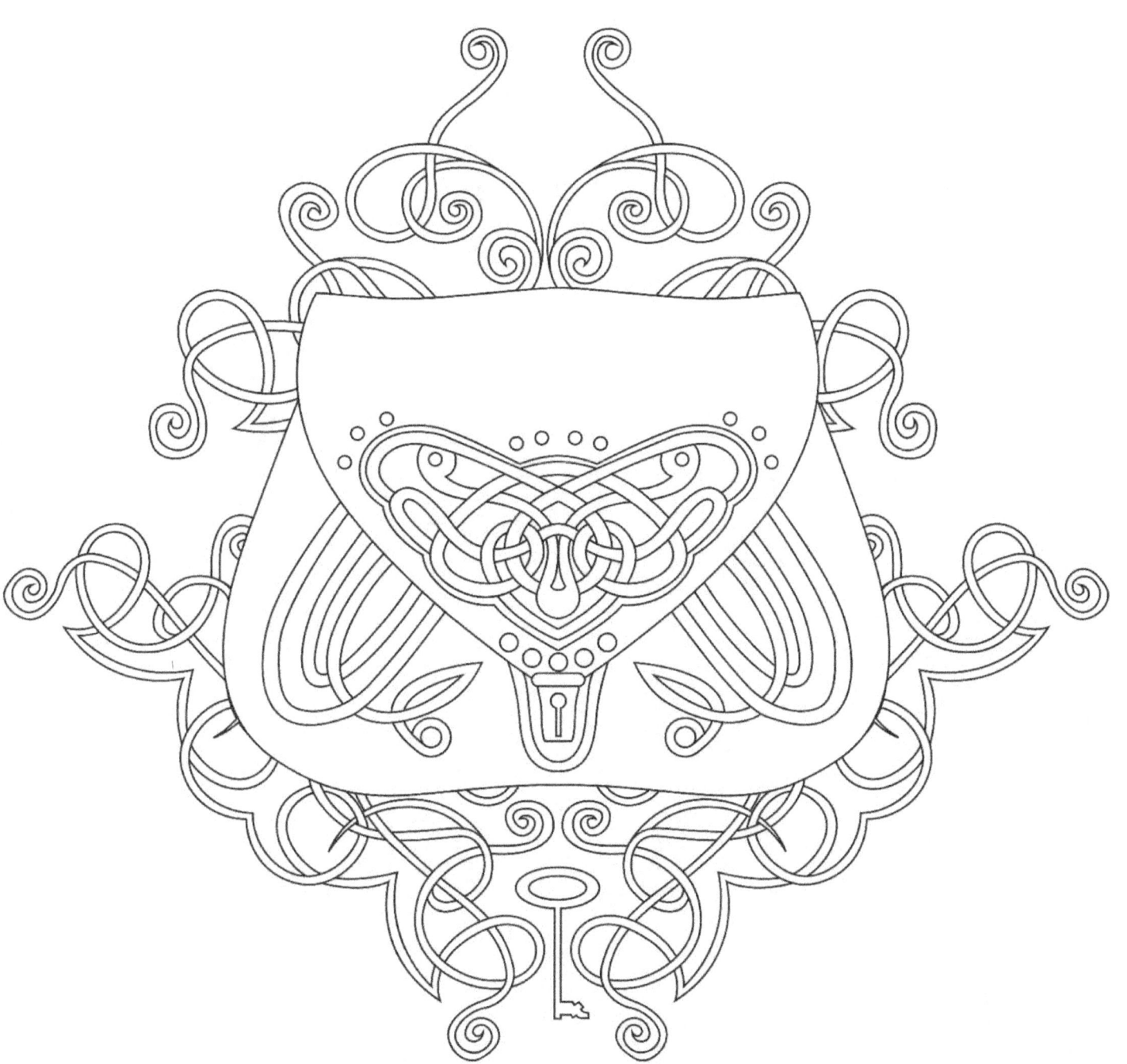

What You Think About Becomes Reality: It's important to keep track of your thoughts, because where you focus your mental energy, whether positive or negative, becomes your reality. This isn't magic, it's logic. For example, if you're thinking someone doesn't care about you, you're going to behave differently around them, and likely bring about the negative result just by thinking that way. Always think positively.

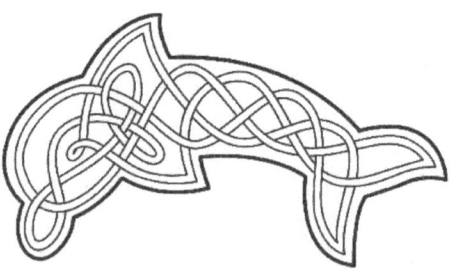

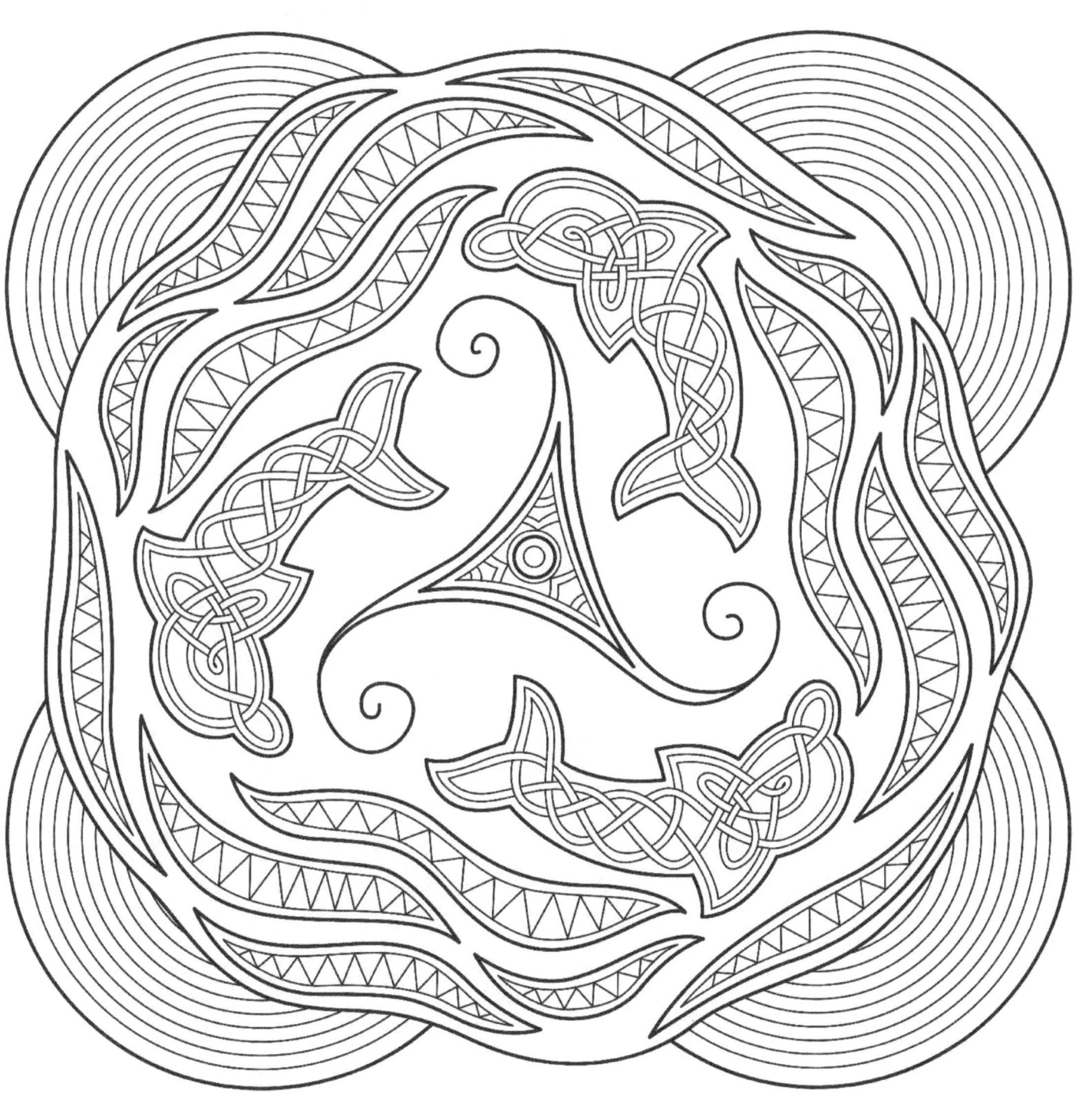

Never Loan Money: Loaning money to friends and family will cause strained relationships, especially if they're slow paying it back. To save relationships, don't loan money to people you love unless you can afford to give it away. Then, instead of loaning it, tell them it's a gift that they can repay if they are ever able to, but not to worry about it. Some day it may come back to you, but until it does simply forget about it.

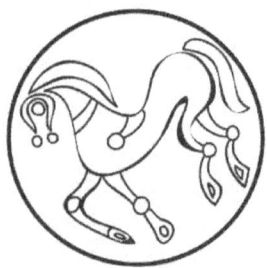

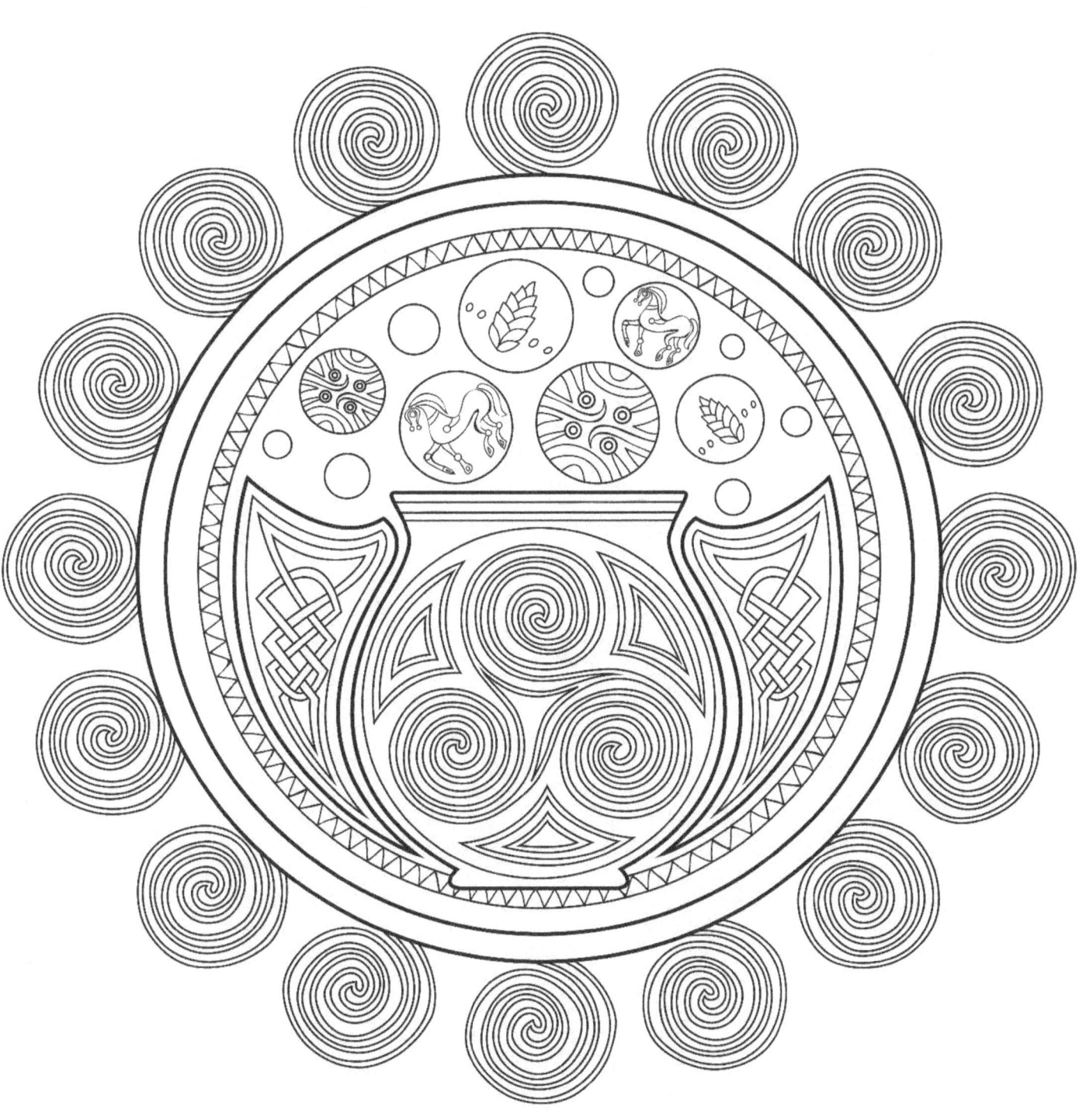

We All Need Help Sometimes: Don't be too proud to ask for help. We all need help sometimes. That's what friends and families do for each other.

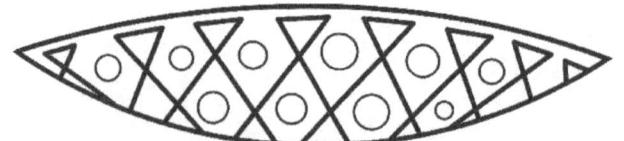

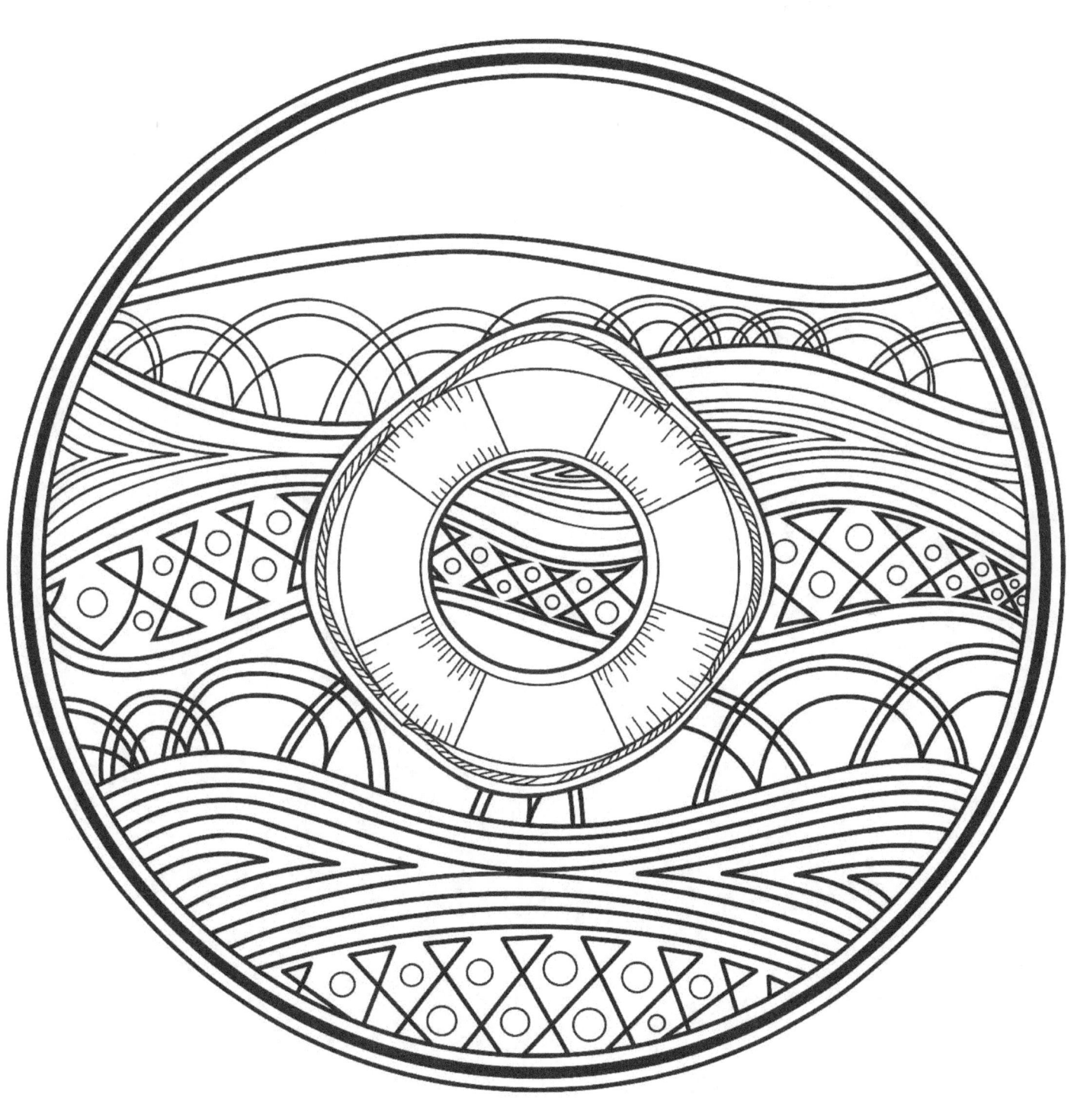

Prepare For Rainy Days: Into each life some rain will fall! It's better to be ready. Make sure you put some money away so you have more choices when it happens.

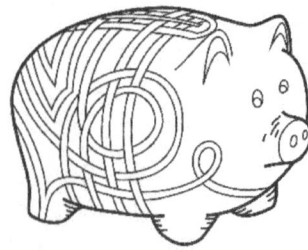

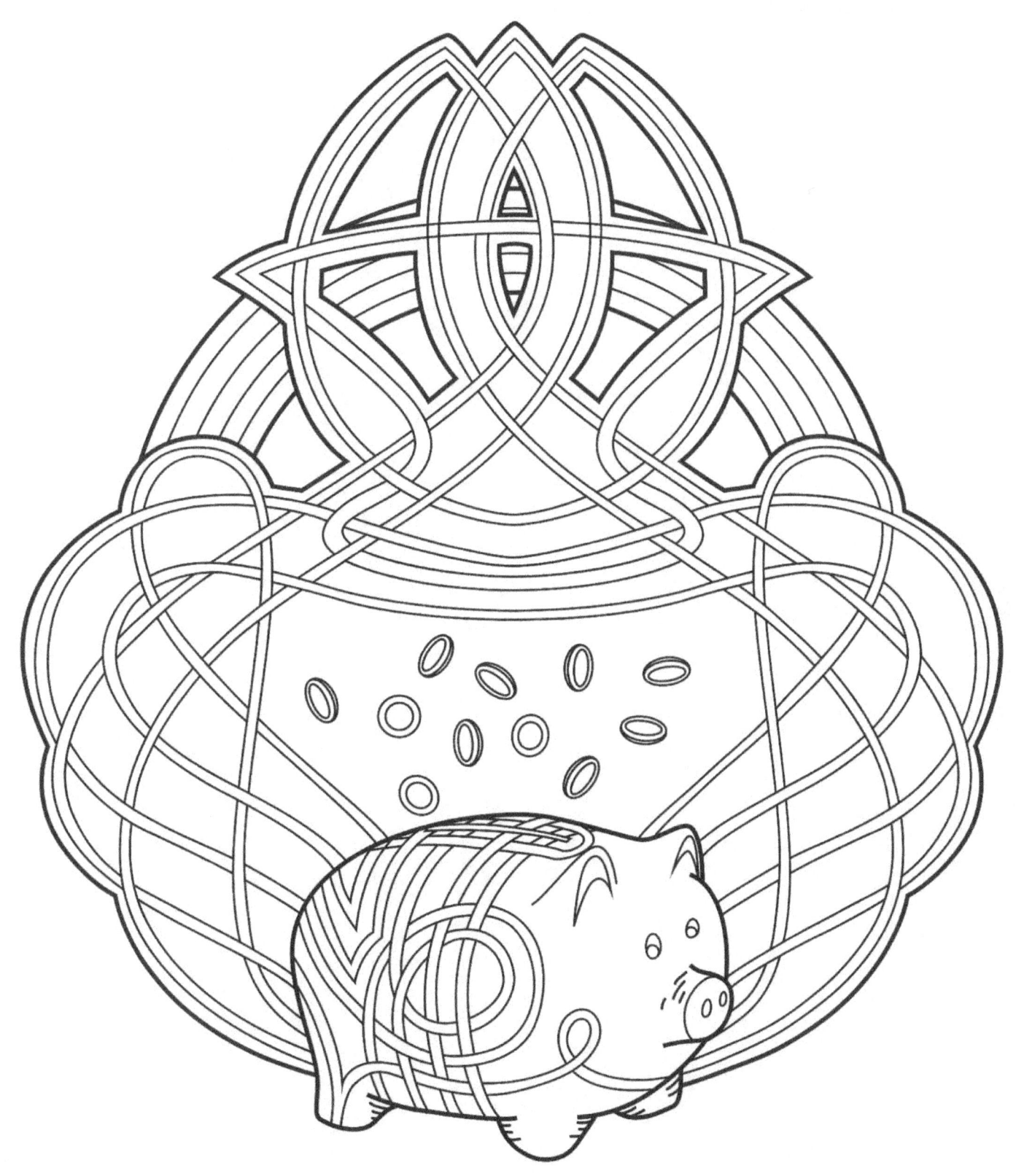

FollowYour Dreams: Life is too short to spend years doing something you don't love. Follow your dreams.

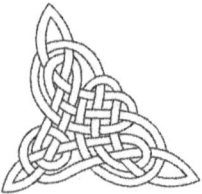

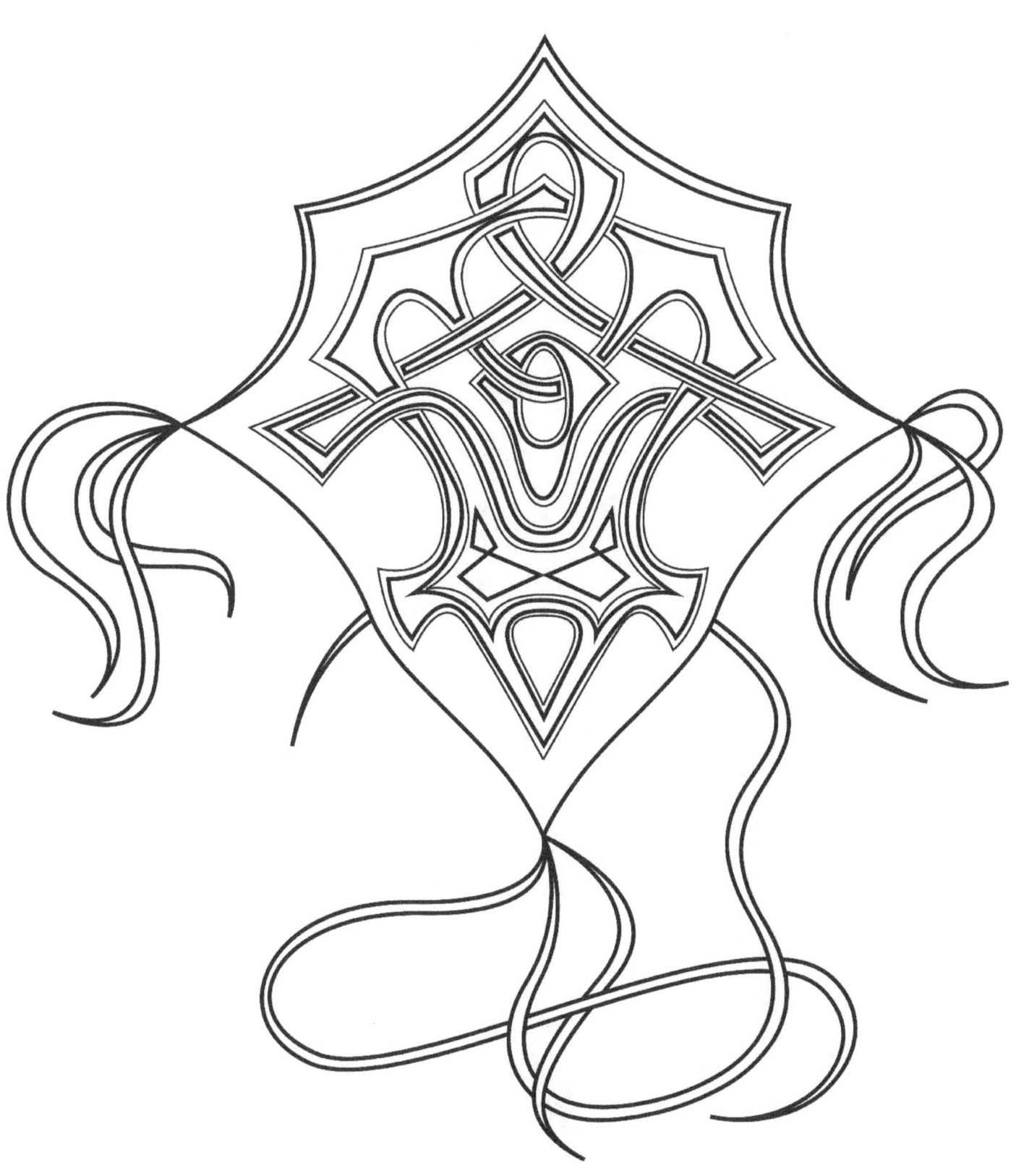

Be Happy: Happiness is a choice we make every day. You may not be able to choose some of the things that happen in your life, but you can choose how you think and feel about them. Focus on positive, focus on happy.

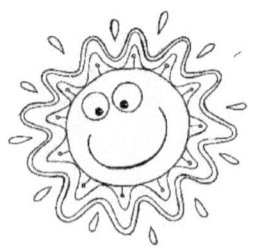

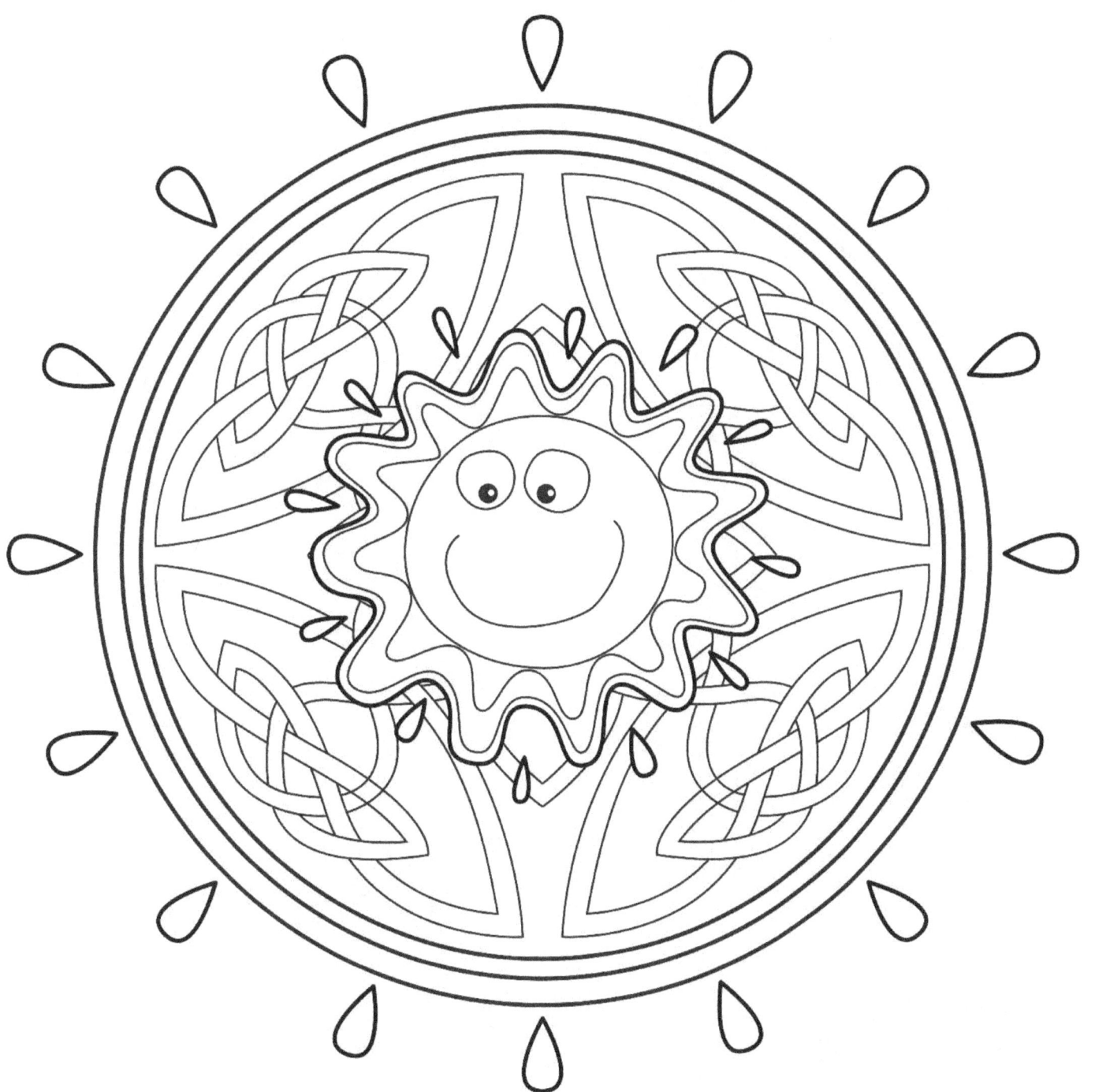

You Are Loved: If you feel alone or unloved remember that someone, somewhere loves you, even if you have not met them yet. <3

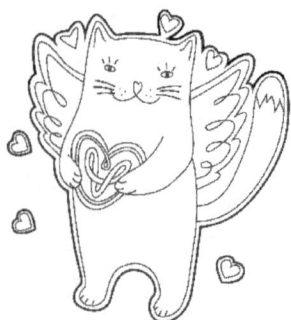

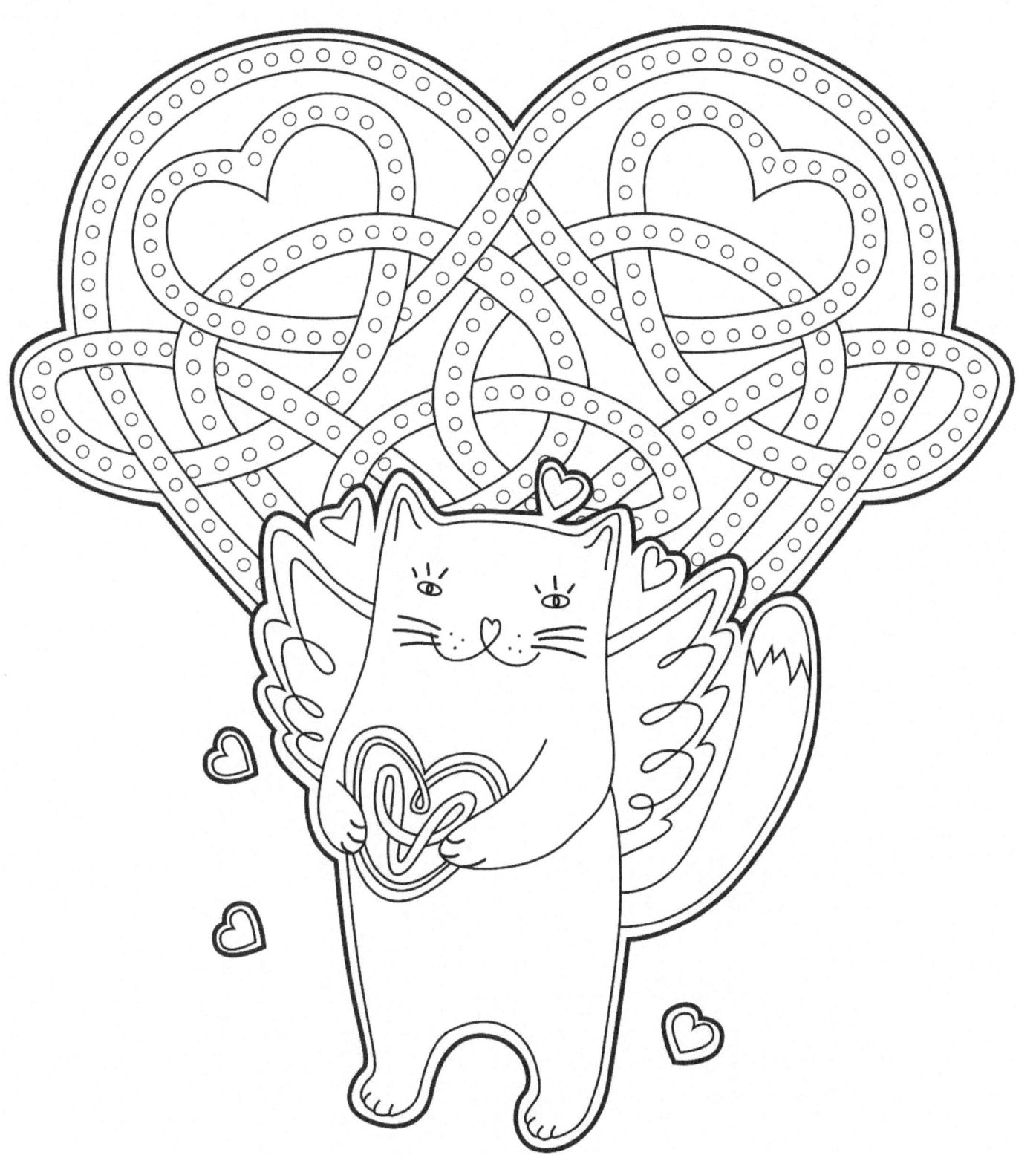

I hope you have enjoyed coloring The Wisdom of Mom, and that the pictures and words in it have brought you some joy.

If you love this book, I would ask a favor of you… Please take a moment and leave positive feedback on Amazon.com for me, as many people use that feedback in their decision to buy a book. Thank You!

If you don't love this book, please let me know what I could have done better. You can reach me through **WisdomOfMom.com.**

To sign up for our mailing list, go to WisdomOfMom.com and click the link there.

Other Books by Audrey O'Shea:

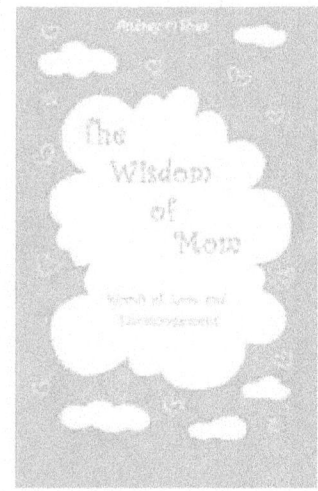

The Wisdom of Mom: Words of Love and Encouragement
ISBN: 1530297753   ISBN13: 978-1530297757

Available through Amazon.com, Barnes and Noble.com, and many other book sellers.

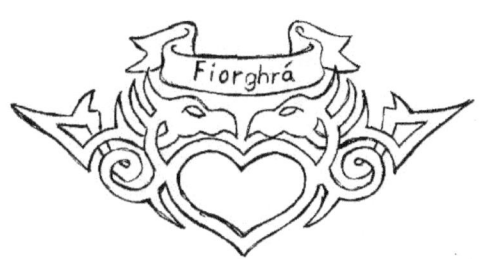

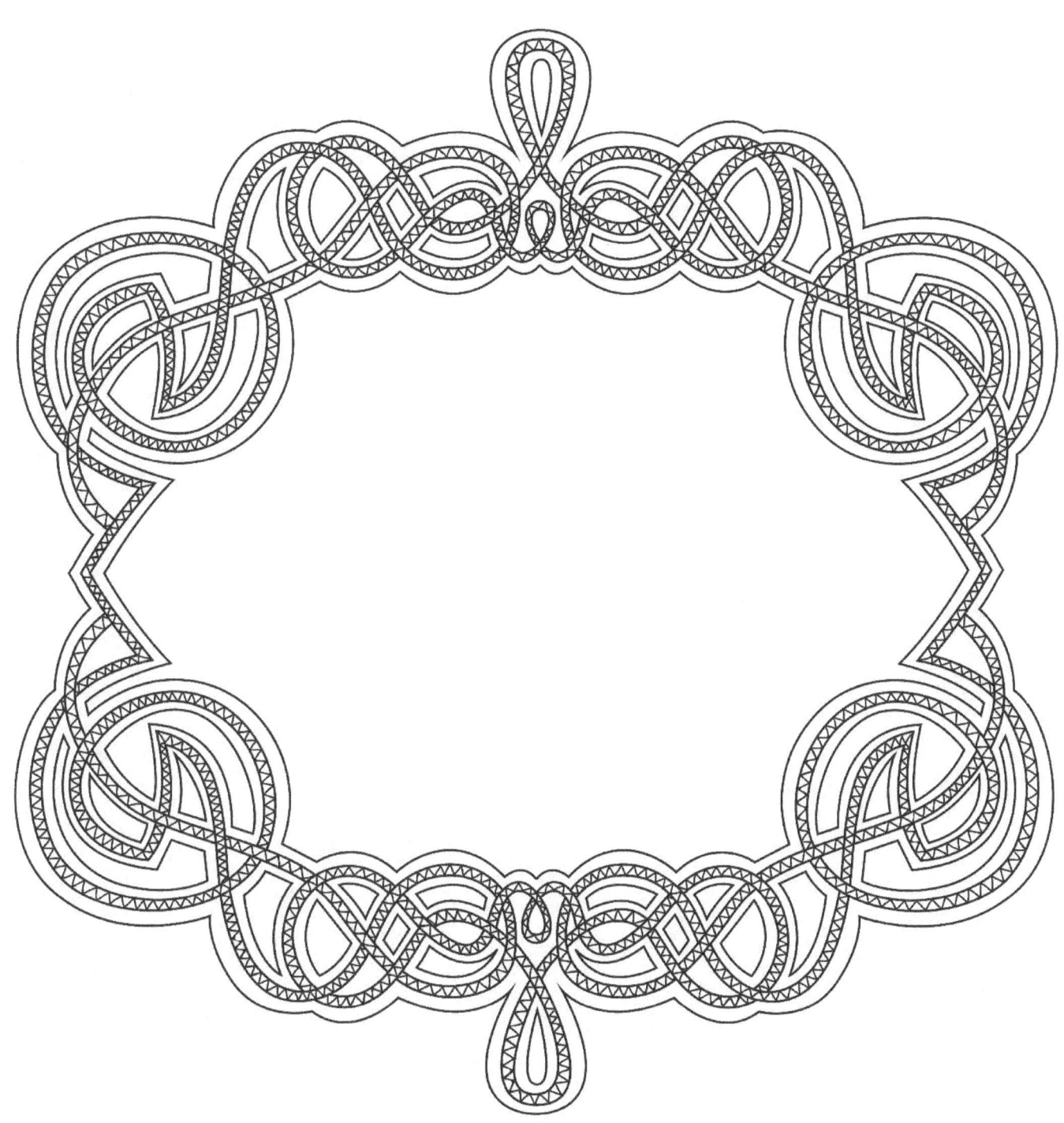

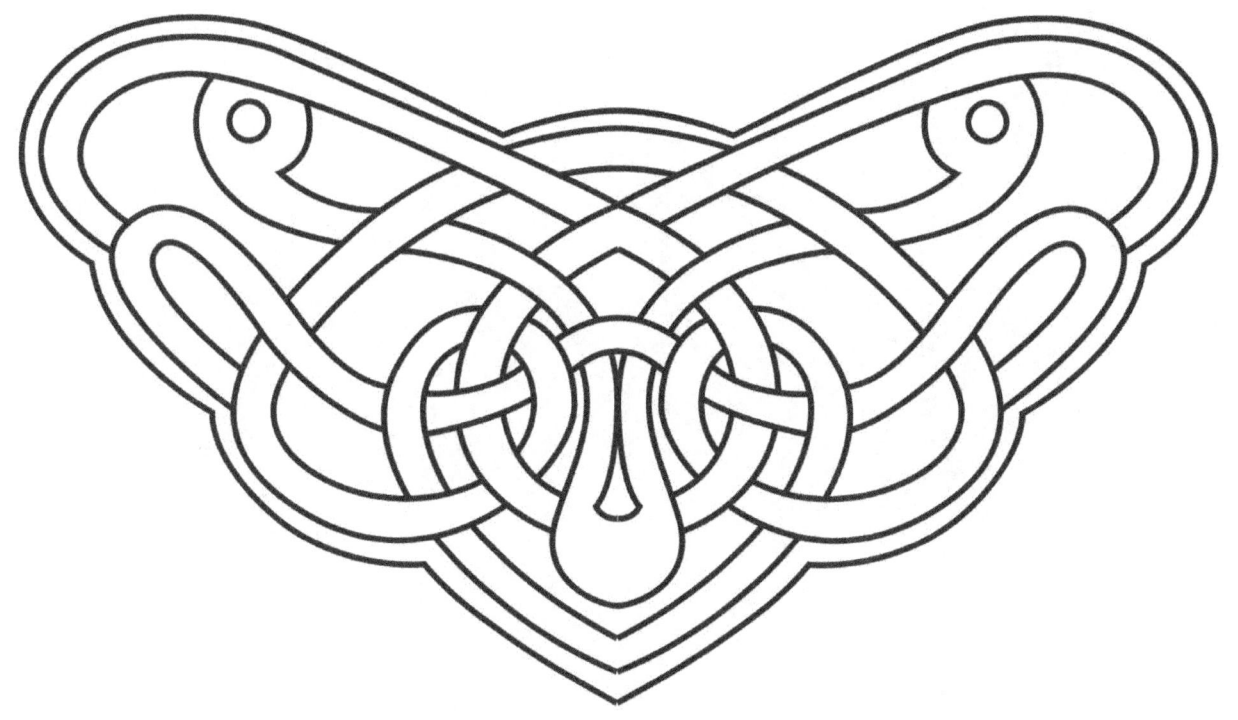

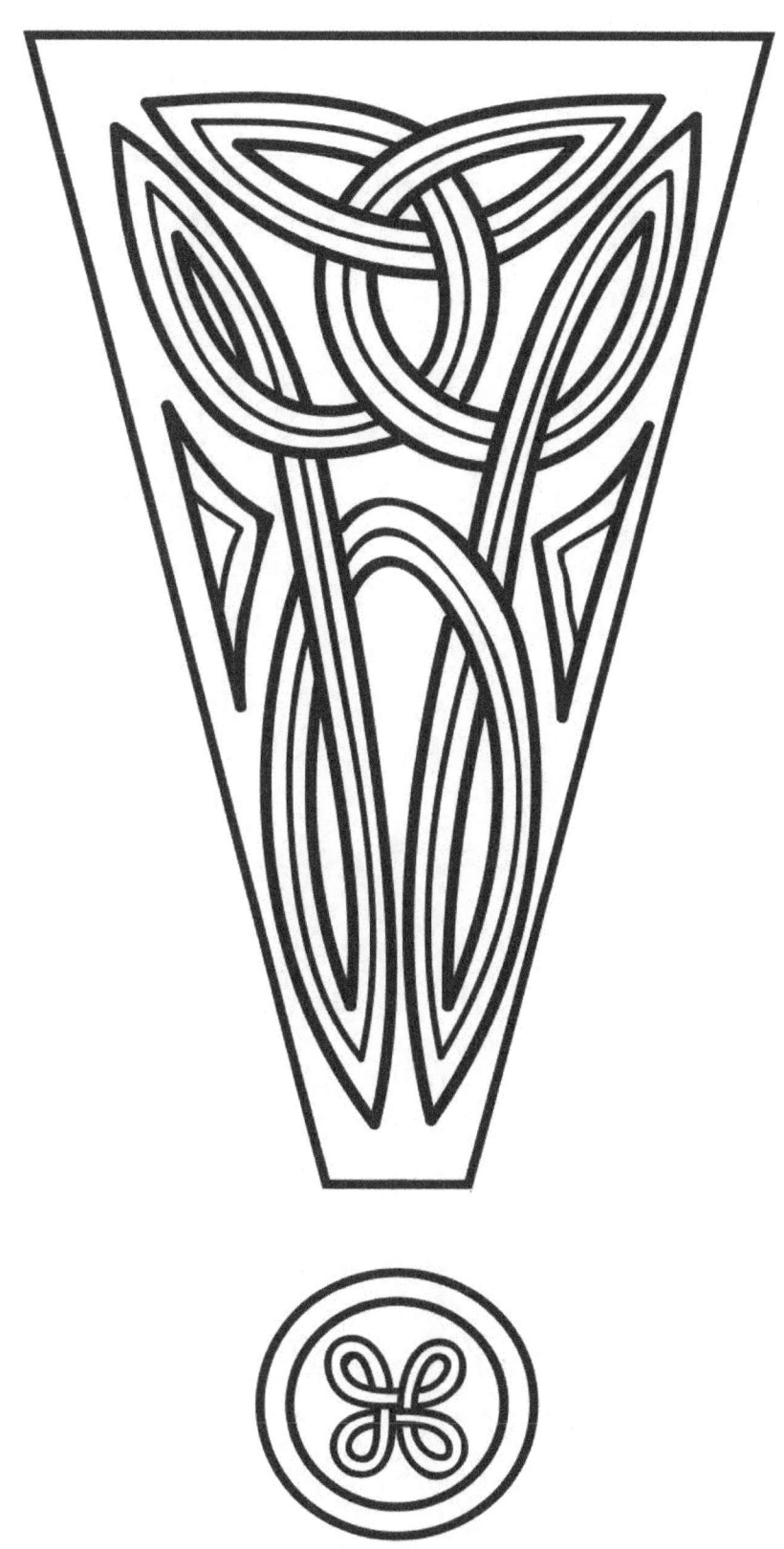